Full Stack Web Development: Build Seamless User Experiences

Master Front-End and Back-End Development Techniques

Oliver Sutherland

Table of Contents

INTRODUCTION

Full-stack web development has emerged as one of the most in-demand competencies in today's digital environment. The need for developers with the ability to effectively combine front-end and back-end systems to produce scalable, effective, and user-friendly online applications is greater than ever as technology advances. "Full Stack Web Development: Build Seamless User Experiences: Master Front-End and Back-End Development Techniques," is the book you need to learn the ins and outs of full stack engineering.

The technical intricacies of back-end architecture and the artistic accuracy of front-end design are reconciled in this thorough guide. Whether you are a newbie entering the field of web development or an experienced expert looking to improve your abilities, this book gives you the information and resources you need to be successful.

This book goes beyond the basics to cover important subjects like state management, deployment tactics, API creation, and performance optimization to provide flawless user experiences.

You will learn how to create a web application that stands out by striking a balance between functionality, security, and design through concise explanations, useful insights, and real-world examples. You will have the self-assurance to take on full-stack projects and develop web applications that satisfy the needs of contemporary users by the end of this journey.

CHAPTER I
Full Stack Development Overview

What is Full Stack?

The process of developing, administering, and maintaining software or web applications that integrate both the front-end and back-end layers of technology is known as full-stack development. With this all-encompassing method of software development, engineers have the abilities and know-how to manage every facet of the project. Fundamentally, full stack development entails working with both the server-side infrastructure, which guarantees functioning, data management, and communication between different components, and the client-facing side of apps, which users interact with. The phrase "full stack" refers to the capacity to oversee the complete "stack" of technologies that make up a software program.

A web application's front end also referred to as the client side, is in charge of providing an intuitive user experience. Here, users use browsers to engage with the program by navigating sites, clicking buttons, and completing forms. The main front-end technologies are JavaScript, HTML, and CSS. JavaScript adds dynamic elements and interactivity, CSS handles layout and styling, while HTML gives a page structure. React, Angular, and Vue.js are examples of contemporary frameworks and libraries that have further revolutionized front-end development by increasing its efficiency, modularity, and scalability. By making client-side data and event processing easier, these tools enable developers to produce incredibly responsive and dynamic user experiences.

The server side, or back-end, of a web application, on the other hand, manages the back-end operations that enable the front end. Database management, user request processing, business logic execution, and facilitating safe and effective client-server connections are all part of it. Programming languages and frameworks like Node.js, Python, Ruby on Rails, Java, and PHP are essential to back-end development because they let programmers create reliable server-side applications. Furthermore, databases are essential for storing and retrieving data for the application. These databases might be relational (like MySQL and PostgreSQL) or non-relational (like MongoDB). Implementing APIs (Application Programming Interfaces), which enable smooth data interchange and interaction between the front end and the server, is another duty of back-end developers.

The integration of the front end and back end to produce unified and effective apps is the foundation of full-stack development. Because of their diverse skill set, full-stack developers are able to bridge the gap between these two tiers. They can easily handle the difficulties of integration since they are aware of the complexities on both sides. A full-stack developer might, for instance, combine React to create an aesthetically pleasing user interface and Node.js to create an API that retrieves and displays real-time data. In addition to expediting the development process, this capacity to work on both sides of the application guarantees improved teamwork and communication.

The increasing need for flexible developers who can adjust to different project needs has contributed to the growth of full-stack development. Full-stack engineers are now extremely valuable in an era of startups and rapid development, where resources are frequently scarce. Because they can do a variety of tasks, less specialized developers are required for each stack layer because full-stack developers may contribute to both the technical and artistic sides of a project, offering a more comprehensive perspective. This versatility also fosters higher innovation.

Creating smooth user experiences is one of the main advantages of full-stack development. Full-stack developers may make sure that the front end and back end function together by comprehending the entire development process. For example, they can create a database schema that satisfies the requirements of the user interface or optimize API answers to enhance a web page's performance. Developers are able to produce programs that are not only useful but also simple to use and intuitive because of this end-to-end expertise.

Full-stack development has its share of difficulties. Full-stack developers must become proficient in a wide variety of tools and technologies, which can be daunting. It takes constant learning and flexibility to stay current with the newest frameworks, trends, and best practices in front-end and back-end development. Full-stack developers also need to be skilled in problem-solving and debugging because problems can occur at any stack tier. Notwithstanding these difficulties, becoming proficient in full-stack development has several benefits, including the ability to take on a variety of worthwhile projects and a wide range of employment options.

Along with traditional web development, full-stack skills are becoming more and more important in cutting-edge domains like artificial intelligence, cloud computing, and mobile app development. For instance, a lot of mobile applications use a mix of back-end services and front-end frameworks to provide functions like user authentication, data synchronization, and push notifications. Likewise, full-stack developers are essential to the development of cloud-based applications that make use of distributed databases and scalable server infrastructures. Full-stack developers are looking for ways to include intelligent features like chatbots, recommendation engines, and predictive analytics into web apps as AI and machine learning continue to advance.

Learning the foundations of front-end and back-end development is usually the first step toward becoming a full-stack developer. Aspiring developers frequently begin by creating simple web pages using HTML, CSS, and JavaScript before progressively progressing to more complex ideas like state management, responsive design, and component-based architecture. They get knowledge of database administration, server-side programming, and API development on the back end. In order to maintain code integrity and collaborate on projects, many developers also learn how to use version control systems like Git.

In addition to technical expertise, full-stack development calls for a collaborative mentality, excellent problem-solving skills, and good communication. The capacity to interact with team members, troubleshoot problems and convey ideas is essential for developers, who frequently work in teams to complete complicated projects. Additionally, full-stack developers must exercise critical and creative thinking in order to create solutions that satisfy user requirements while staying within technical limitations.

Mastering technologies is simply one aspect of full-stack development; another is embracing an attitude of flexibility and constant progress. Because it takes constant work to be relevant in a world where new frameworks, programming languages, and approaches appear on a regular basis, the function of a full-stack developer is dynamic. For instance, although JavaScript continues to be a fundamental component of front-end development, the frameworks that use it, such as React, Angular, and Vue.js, have changed dramatically over time, adding capabilities like hooks, virtual DOMs, and modular components. The deployment and scaling of apps have also been altered on the back end by serverless architectures and containerization tools like Docker and Kubernetes. Adopting these innovations is crucial for full-stack developers to maintain their competitiveness in the market.

The focus on end-to-end responsibility is one of the characteristics that distinguish full-stack development. Front-end and back-end developers frequently work in silos in a conventional software development workflow, which can cause delays, communication breakdowns, and integration issues. However, a full-stack developer has the exceptional capacity to manage every step of the process, from designing the user interface to putting the database structures and server logic into place. This all-encompassing viewpoint guarantees that the finished output is coherent and well-integrated in addition to increasing efficiency.

Beyond their technical proficiency, full-stack developers are versatile. They frequently have to communicate with clients, stakeholders, and team members from different fields, including designers, project managers, and quality assurance testers. In order to bridge the gap between technical and non-technical stakeholders, effective communication and teamwork are essential. For example, a full-stack developer working on an e-commerce platform project would work with a UX designer to build a user-friendly checkout process and with database administrators to guarantee safe and effective payment processing. Full-stack developers are essential in collaborative and fast-paced settings because of their versatility.

The significance of full-stack development has been further increased by the emergence of agile approaches and DevOps methods. Full-stack engineers may adjust to changing priorities and contribute to various regions of the stack in agile development, which emphasizes iterative progress and rapid feedback loops. To expedite the deployment, testing, and monitoring procedures, DevOps, on the other hand, encourages the convergence of development and operations teams. With their wide range of abilities, full-stack engineers are well-suited to flourish in these settings since they can handle a variety of tasks, such as developing code, setting up CI/CD pipelines, and keeping an eye on the performance of applications.

The opportunity for creativity and experimentation that comes with full-stack development is among its most alluring features. To identify the best solutions for a given problem, full-stack developers are allowed to experiment with different tools, test different design patterns, and investigate new technologies and frameworks. For instance, companies could try using progressive web app (PWA) approaches to make an application accessible offline or experimenting with server-side rendering to speed up page loads. In addition to maintaining developer engagement, this innovative culture pushes the limits of web development.

Full-stack development is used in a variety of sectors and use cases in the real world. Full-stack developers are in charge of creating e-commerce platforms that let customers easily browse products, make purchases, and keep track of orders. Another excellent example is social networking platforms, which depend on full-stack development to make features like tailored content feeds, real-time messaging, and user profiles possible. In a similar vein, enterprise software solutions—like human resource management and customer relationship management (CRM) systems—frequently incorporate intricate full-stack frameworks to satisfy the various demands of companies.

Full-stack development has also greatly improved the healthcare and education sectors. For example, full-stack solutions are used by online learning platforms such as Coursera and edX to handle user data, offer interactive courses, and facilitate real-time contact between teachers and students. Applications such as electronic health record systems and telemedicine platforms depend on full-stack developers to build safe and intuitive user interfaces that link patients, physicians, and healthcare providers.

It is impossible to overestimate the importance of full-stack developers in creating scalable and secure apps as the world grows more linked. As the number of Internet of Things (IoT) devices increases, full-stack development is also becoming increasingly important in facilitating communication between software and hardware systems. For instance, full-stack developers are frequently needed for smart home applications in order to create dashboards for device control and oversee the back-end infrastructure that interprets sensor data and issues commands.

Looking ahead, developments in blockchain, AI, and machine learning are probably going to have a significant impact on full-stack development. To improve user experiences, full-stack developers are already experimenting with chatbots, recommendation engines, and predictive analytics driven by AI. Developers are creating decentralized apps (dApps) in the blockchain realm that use distributed ledgers and smart contracts to facilitate safe and open transactions. For full-stack engineers, these new technologies present exciting chances to push boundaries and have a significant influence.

To sum up, full-stack development is an exciting and fulfilling industry that blends problem-solving, technological know-how, and creativity. Full-stack developers can produce applications that foster creativity and offer flawless user experiences by being proficient in both the front-end and back-end facets of web development. Whether you're creating a basic website or a sophisticated web application, the full-stack development principles offer a strong basis for success in the rapidly changing technological landscape.

Modern Technology Stack

Contemporary technology stacks serve as the foundation for software development, allowing companies and developers to produce reliable, scalable, and effective programs that are adapted to customers' changing needs. Essentially, a technology stack is a group of programming languages, frameworks, tools, and libraries that cooperate to create, implement, and manage software solutions. These stacks are made up of multiple layers, each of which is in charge of different facets of the functionality of the program, such as the databases, infrastructure, front end, and back end. The rapid increase of computing capabilities over time has coincided with the evolution of technology stacks, bringing about a new era of highly specialized and integrated solutions that have completely changed the software development lifecycle.

With an emphasis on providing outstanding user experiences, the front-end layer of a contemporary technological stack has experienced a substantial transition. The foundation of front-end development is now made up of frameworks like React, Angular, and Vue.js, which enable programmers to create responsive, interactive, and aesthetically pleasing user interfaces. To improve performance and expedite the development process, these frameworks make use of features like virtual DOMs, component-based designs, and state management systems. Furthermore, responsive and mobile-first design ideas are embraced by contemporary front-end technology, guaranteeing smooth interoperability on a variety of screens and devices. The distinction between web and mobile platforms is becoming increasingly hazy with the introduction of progressive web applications (PWAs), which allow developers to produce web apps that offer native-like experiences, replete with offline capabilities and push notifications.

The back end is in charge of the processes and logic that drive applications, whereas the front end concentrates on user engagement. The usage of flexible and fast frameworks such as Node.js, Django, Ruby on Rails, and Spring Boot is a hallmark of contemporary back-end development. These frameworks give programmers the resources and tools they need to create scalable server-side apps that can manage intricate data processing and workflow processes. Because of its non-blocking I/O approach, which makes it easy for developers to manage concurrent requests, Node.js, in particular, has become incredibly popular. The incorporation of asynchronous programming paradigms, which enable back-end systems to maintain responsiveness even under demanding workloads, significantly increases this efficiency.

Databases are essential components of contemporary technology stacks because they provide the framework for data storage and retrieval. The type of application and its particular needs determine which database is best. Because of their organized data structures, capacity to handle sophisticated queries, and adherence to the ACID (Atomicity, Consistency, Isolation, Durability) principles, relational databases like MySQL, PostgreSQL, and Microsoft SQL Server have long been preferred. However, developers now have scalable and adaptable options for managing unstructured and semi-structured data thanks to the emergence of NoSQL databases like MongoDB, Cassandra, and DynamoDB. In use cases where data volumes and diversity might be daunting, such as real-time analytics, content management, and Internet of Things (IoT) applications, NoSQL databases are especially well-suited.

By giving developers access to on-demand resources and services, cloud computing has completely transformed the infrastructure layer of technology stacks, doing away with the need for expensive hardware purchases. A wide range of tools are available for hosting, growing, and administering apps in the cloud from platforms including Google Cloud Platform (GCP), Microsoft Azure, and Amazon Web Services (AWS). With the help of these platforms, developers can concentrate on creating apps rather than worrying about the intricacies of the underlying infrastructure. These services include managed databases, serverless computing, virtual machines, and container orchestration. Cloud resource provisioning has become even easier with the use of Infrastructure as Code (IaC) technologies like Terraform and AWS CloudFormation, which enable teams to build and deploy infrastructure in a consistent and repeatable way.

Applications may now be deployed and managed in a variety of contexts thanks to containers and container orchestration, which are now essential parts of contemporary technology stacks. One of the top containerization platforms, Docker, enables developers to bundle apps and their dependencies into portable containers that function uniformly in testing, production, and development settings. The de facto standard for scaling containerized systems is Kubernetes, an open-source container orchestration framework. Kubernetes enables teams to attain high availability and operational efficiency in their deployments with capabilities like rolling updates, self-healing, and autonomous scaling.

Technology stack implementation and maintenance have changed as a result of DevOps principles, which have promoted automation and teamwork. Modern DevOps workflows are characterized by continuous integration and continuous delivery (CI/CD) pipelines, which allow teams to automate integration, deployment, and code testing procedures. Developers can deploy software updates more rapidly and reliably with the help of tools like Jenkins, GitLab CI/CD, and CircleCI, which shorten time-to-market and lower the risks involved with human interventions. Furthermore, Prometheus, Grafana, and Datadog are examples of monitoring and observability technologies that are essential for maintaining the functionality and health of applications by enabling teams to proactively detect and fix problems.

Because cyber threats are becoming more frequent and sophisticated, security has become a top priority when designing current technology stacks. In order to protect apps and user data, developers increasingly incorporate security measures at every stack layer, implementing techniques like secure coding, encryption, and access control. To find and fix such vulnerabilities, web application firewalls (WAFs), intrusion detection systems (IDS), and vulnerability scanning technologies are frequently used. Furthermore, in order to guarantee that applications fulfill strict data protection criteria, adherence to industry standards and laws like GDPR, HIPAA, and ISO 27001 has become a crucial component of technology stack deployment.

Within contemporary technological stacks, artificial intelligence (AI) and machine learning (ML) have become revolutionary forces that allow apps to provide intelligent and personalized experiences. With the aid of frameworks like TensorFlow, PyTorch, and Scikit-learn, developers can create and implement machine learning models that are capable of analyzing large datasets, spotting trends, and formulating predictions. Natural language processing (NLP), computer vision, and recommendation systems are examples of AI-driven features that have proliferated, improving user engagement and generating commercial results. Because developers must make sure that their solutions are impartial, transparent, and equitable, integrating AI and ML into technology stacks calls for both technical know-how and a thorough grasp of ethical issues.

The emergence of contemporary technology stacks is evidence of the software development community's inventiveness and flexibility. Developers are always looking for new and creative methods to improve the functionality, scalability, and efficiency of their stacks as new technologies and paradigms keep emerging. The possibilities are endless, whether it's through the usage of augmented reality (AR) and virtual reality (VR) for immersive experiences, the use of edge computing to lower latency, or the deployment of blockchain for safe transactions. Building and maintaining a contemporary technological stack involves ongoing learning and exploration, motivated by a common goal of expanding the capabilities of technology.

The idea of the "stack" becomes more complicated as contemporary technology develops further, including a wide range of tools, services, and platforms that cooperate to produce creative, adaptable, and scalable applications. Navigating the wide range of technologies available and choosing the best set of tools to match project objectives, team capabilities, and user expectations is one of the biggest problems facing developers today. Integrating contemporary technology stacks has become not only essential but also a competitive advantage in the industry as companies work to satisfy the always-rising demands of their clientele.

Microservices have also gained prominence in contemporary technological stacks. Developers can divide large, monolithic programs into more manageable, self-contained services that can be independently created, implemented, and expanded thanks to microservices design. Teams can work on separate application components concurrently with this modular approach, increasing development speed and flexibility. Microservices make it simpler to manage and scale services in a cloud-native environment. They are frequently combined with containerization technologies like Docker and coordinated using platforms like Kubernetes. Organizations can improve system stability, increase fault tolerance, and speed up the rollout of updates and new features by implementing microservices.

A new paradigm for creating scalable applications has also been made possible by the emergence of serverless computing, which has further transformed contemporary technology stacks. With a serverless paradigm, developers don't have to worry about the underlying infrastructure and can concentrate solely on creating application logic. Developers no longer need to maintain servers thanks to services like AWS Lambda, Azure Functions, and Google Cloud Functions, which scale dynamically in response to the volume of incoming requests. By just paying for the precise amount of computing power they utilize, this move to serverless computing allows businesses to save expenses while also speeding up development. Serverless computing does, however, necessitate rigorous application design consideration to guarantee that features are effective, maintainable, and able to manage a variety of workloads.

The emergence of API-driven architectures is another noteworthy development in contemporary technology stacks. Application Programming Interfaces, or APIs, have long been crucial for facilitating data sharing and communication across various software systems. APIs have grown even more crucial in the context of contemporary technological stacks, enabling interoperability across various platforms and services.

GraphQL, gRPC, and RESTful APIs are some of the most popular API architectures; each has unique benefits based on the use case. Because of their popularity and ease of use, RESTful APIs are a popular alternative for online and mobile apps. However, GraphQL provides a more adaptable querying strategy that minimizes over-fetching and under-fetching by enabling clients to request precisely the data they require. The capacity to provide reliable, scalable, and secure APIs has become essential to modern technology stacks as companies depend more and more on third-party services and interfaces.

Additionally, machine learning (ML) and artificial intelligence (AI) have established themselves at the center of contemporary technology stacks. AI and ML are becoming indispensable technologies in the developer's toolbox because of the increasing demand for automation, intelligent decision-making, and personalized user experiences. AI has the potential to revolutionize a variety of industries, whether it is through allowing autonomous systems, evaluating customer sentiment through natural language processing, or utilizing machine learning algorithms to suggest products on an e-commerce website. Cloud-based systems like AWS SageMaker, Google AI, and Azure Machine Learning offer the infrastructure required to deploy, monitor, and scale these models, while frameworks like TensorFlow, PyTorch, and Keras make it simple for developers to create complex AI and ML models. The integration of AI and ML into contemporary technology stacks will only grow as companies continue to engage in data-driven decision-making, allowing them to remain competitive and provide their clients with cutting-edge solutions.

Alongside these technical developments, data security and privacy have taken center stage in the creation of contemporary technology stacks. Developers must incorporate strong security measures into each tier of the technological stack due to the rising frequency of cyberattacks and data breaches. To safeguard sensitive data, this includes intrusion detection, identity and access management (IAM), encryption, and secure APIs. A crucial component of contemporary software development is adherence to laws like the CCPA, GDPR, and HIPAA, especially when working with personal data. Organizations may protect their applications from threats and foster user trust by integrating security principles into the development lifecycle. Additionally, using encryption technologies like public-key infrastructure (PKI) and end-to-end encryption guarantees that data is safe while being stored or transported.

Modern technology stacks will continue to change as we go forward in response to shifting company objectives, technical breakthroughs, and user needs. The design and implementation of technological stacks will be impacted by the quick speed of innovation in fields like 5G, blockchain, augmented reality (AR), virtual reality (VR), and edge computing. Edge computing, for instance, will make it possible to process data closer to the point of origin, lowering latency and enabling real-time applications that can operate in settings with spotty or limited connectivity. The creation of immersive experiences that combine the real and virtual worlds will be made possible by the incorporation of AR and VR into technological stacks, opening up new markets in industries like gaming, healthcare, education, and retail. Blockchain is expected to be crucial in industries including finance, supply chain management, and digital identity management since it promises decentralized, safe, and transparent transactions.

At the same time, developers will need to reconsider conventional methods of software architecture due to the growing dependence on distributed systems and cloud infrastructure. Hybrid and multi-cloud techniques are growing in popularity as businesses look to cut expenses, lessen vendor lock-in, and boost redundancy. The rise of quantum computing also has the potential to change how technology stacks develop in the future by providing fresh approaches to challenging issues that are currently outside the purview of traditional computing systems. But like other new technologies, quantum computing has implementation, scalability, and security issues, and it will probably take years before it is widely used in contemporary technological stacks.

Collaboration, creativity, and a thorough awareness of the tools at hand, as well as the particular requirements of the company or organization, will be necessary to integrate these disparate technologies into coherent, scalable, and effective stacks. The function of the full-stack developer will change in tandem with the complexity and specialization of technology stacks. In addition to being proficient in front-end and back-end technologies, full-stack engineers should also be well-versed in cloud services, containerization, microservices, APIs, security, and AI/ML. Developers will also need to embrace new processes and toolkits that prioritize cooperation, speed, and dependability due to the increasing significance of DevOps approaches, automation, and continuous integration/continuous deployment (CI/CD) pipelines.

To sum up, contemporary technology stacks are leading the way in the digital revolution that is changing how consumers and organizations use technology. The elements of a contemporary technology stack are numerous and varied, ranging from cloud platforms and containerization to artificial intelligence and microservices, each of which contributes in a different way to the creation of innovative applications. Organizations may create software that is secure, scalable, and capable of meeting users' changing needs by carefully choosing and integrating the appropriate tools, frameworks, and services. The technologies that support contemporary stacks will change along with the technological world, providing both developers and companies with exciting new prospects. Anyone hoping to remain competitive in the fast-paced field of software development, where creativity and adaptability are essential for success, must comprehend the complexities of contemporary technological stacks.

Why Seamless Integration Matters

Seamless integration in full-stack web development is crucial to building modern, scalable, and efficient applications. The need for developing systems that function flawlessly throughout the front-end, back-end, and database layers of the stack has increased dramatically as web development has progressed over time. A web application's user interface (UI), server-side logic, database interactions, and even deployment are all under the purview of full-stack developers. With more interactive features, real-time data syncing, and third-party integrations, web applications have become more sophisticated. As a result, guaranteeing smooth integration between every component of the stack is now essential to attaining effectiveness, scalability, and a satisfying user experience rather than being a choice.

When every element of the stack—from the front-end programming to the databases and back-end infrastructure—works in unison, it's referred to as a seamless integration. The mechanisms that enable communication between servers, databases, and the client's browser are also included in this integration. An application's overall performance and usability are influenced by the data flow, layer-to-layer interactions, and reaction time. The end-user experience will suffer if any of these elements are unable to communicate effectively or cause friction while managing data, which could result in problems, poorer performance, or even the failure of the program altogether.

With the introduction of new technology and approaches in recent years, web development has undergone substantial change. When the internet first started, developers mostly concentrated on one side of the stack, making the distinction between front-end and back-end development more obvious. But as websites got more dynamic and interactive, it became clear that front-end and back-end technology needed to be seamlessly integrated. Developers may now create applications with full-stack capabilities, which include managing data storage and retrieval as well as processing user input. But with this, increased accountability also comes the difficulty of making sure that front-end and back-end components interact seamlessly, quickly, and without problems.

Typically, front-end or client-side web development uses frameworks like React, Angular, and Vue.js together with technologies like HTML, CSS, and JavaScript. Users interact directly with this interface. Front-end developers are in charge of making sure the user interface (UI) is responsive, visually appealing, and simple to use. But without back-end assistance, the front-end can only accomplish so much. Languages like Python, Ruby, Java, PHP, or Node.js power the back end, which communicates with databases, handles user requests and provides dynamic content. There will be delays, misunderstandings, and malfunctions if these two development domains are not coordinated.

Think of a normal web application user experience. When a button is clicked by the user, an action is initiated, such as submitting a form or retrieving data. The back-end server, which processes the data, communicates with the database if required, and finally replies to the front-end, must be triggered by this user action. Slow response times or improperly structured data might irritate users, which can lower their level of happiness or possibly cause them to stop using the service. Here's when smooth integration is important. Full-stack developers need to make sure that front-end and back-end communication is effective, optimized, and error-free in order to produce a flawless user experience.

The significance of smooth integration goes beyond the application's user interface. Integrating external libraries, APIs, and third-party services into the system is another aspect of full-stack web development. APIs are frequently used by contemporary web applications for functions including data storage, email sending, payment processing, and authentication. These integrations need to be done properly, whether they include merging with social networking sites like Facebook or Twitter or dealing with cloud-based services like AWS and Google Cloud. If this isn't done, there may be security flaws, user data corruption, or an inability to access outside resources. An application can reply to queries, manage user requests in real time, and provide content with ease when a full-stack developer makes sure that databases, server-side logic, and APIs all work together effortlessly.

Furthermore, application performance is greatly impacted by smooth integration. Optimizing the front-end, back-end, and database interface is crucial since web users expect real-time feedback and responses while interacting with apps. The smooth experience that customers require is facilitated by caching, data processing techniques, server-side rendering (SSR), and client-side rendering (CSR). High availability, faster content delivery, and significantly shorter load times are all possible with a well-integrated architecture. Data flows more effectively between the front-end and back-end when the application's layers cooperate, allowing for quicker updates and a more seamless user experience overall.

The smooth integration also makes debugging and error management easier. A communication problem across the various tiers of the technology stack is frequently the cause of an application's malfunction. Inconsistencies in the data sent between components or communication hurdles can make debugging a nightmare. Developers can find and address problems faster and more efficiently if they make sure that every tier of the stack integrates properly. Furthermore, a coherent stack makes it more probable that issues will be contained inside a single component (either the front-end, back-end, or data storage) as opposed to being dispersed throughout various components, which can make troubleshooting and solution implementation more difficult.

Scalability is another important factor in large-scale applications. Applications that need to scale—either vertically by upgrading hardware or horizontally by adding more servers—benefit from smooth integration. A well-integrated system makes scalability easier to handle since system-to-system communication stays constant as the infrastructure expands. For example, when more people engage with the program, a system that uses a single database server may experience performance problems. However, developers may guarantee that data handling continues without interruption as the program grows by incorporating database sharding or using a distributed database architecture.

Another important factor that contributes to the necessity of seamless integration is security. The surface area for possible security flaws increases as applications get more intricate and incorporate more services. Web applications with fragmented communication between components or inadequate integration are more vulnerable to breaches because attackers can take advantage of inconsistent data handling or transmission practices. By guaranteeing that data is appropriately authenticated, encrypted, and sanitized at every stage of the application's operation, seamless integration helps reduce these risks. In order to ensure that security methods like authorization, authentication, and data encryption are enforced consistently throughout the application, full-stack developers must be careful to secure all layers of the stack.

Continuous delivery and deployment (or CD) also depend on seamless integration. The capacity to provide updates regularly is essential to modern development approaches because it guarantees that bugs are repaired, new features are implemented, and performance is continuously improved. Updates to the front-end, back-end, or any other part of the system won't cause the application to malfunction if the full stack is properly integrated. Automated tests and integration checks, which are essential to CI/CD pipelines, can only function well when the system's components are interdependent. Development teams may improve productivity, optimize workflows, and guarantee that the application stays stable even with frequent changes by implementing a well-integrated full-stack.

It is impossible to overestimate the significance of seamless integration as companies depend more and more on web applications to communicate with clients and spur expansion. A web application's ability to deliver a consistent, responsive, and user-friendly experience is crucial to its success. Developers can produce apps that satisfy user expectations through seamless integration, whether it be through dependable data handling, quick load times, or easy navigation. In order to offer real-time data, maintain performance, and guarantee the stability of the application, it is also necessary to integrate different back-end services, APIs, and external libraries in an effective manner.

Furthermore, as new tools and technologies are developed, the necessity of seamless integration will continue to be emphasized in the future of full-stack development. In order to create scalable, maintainable, and high-performance applications, developers will need to combine progressively more sophisticated technologies, from serverless computing and microservices architectures to the expanding use of containerization and Kubernetes. Seamless integration will continue to be one of the most important aspects of making sure that online apps function properly and offer consumers value as they get increasingly dynamic, data-intensive, and reliant on outside services.

Furthermore, while talking about seamless integration, the importance of cloud computing in full-stack development cannot be emphasized enough. From hosting and storage to machine learning and content delivery networks (CDNs), the cloud provides a wide range of services that need to be integrated with a web application's front-end and back-end components. For instance, developers may implement scalable back-end systems, manage heavy traffic situations, and effectively provide content with the help of cloud services like AWS, Azure, or Google Cloud. By smoothly integrating these services into the stack, the application's performance won't be compromised as its user base grows. Applications that can grow dynamically in response to demand can maintain a seamless user experience even during periods of high traffic.

The way full-stack developers approach seamless integration has also changed as a result of containerization and microservices architectures. Containerized environments, where application components may be segregated, deployed, and scaled independently, have been made possible with the advent of Docker and Kubernetes. Developers may now more easily combine different components of a program while simultaneously encouraging scalability thanks to the microservices architecture, which divides apps into smaller, easier-to-manage services. Because each microservice may be optimized for a particular purpose and run independently of others, this method lowers the possibility of bottlenecks, which are common in monolithic programs. Developers may make sure that the system stays cohesive even when new features or services are added by separating components and integrating them via clear APIs.

The significance of sound testing procedures is another essential component of smooth integration in full-stack web development. Testing ensures that all of the application's parts are functioning as intended, whether they are managing user input on the front end or accessing a database on the back end. Verifying that the integrated system operates as intended involves the use of unit tests, integration tests, and end-to-end tests. Continuously running automated test suites throughout the development cycle is made possible by tools such as PyTest for Python, Mocha for Node.js, and Jest for JavaScript testing. Developers can promptly spot potential integration failure points by automating tests, enabling them to fix problems before they negatively impact the user experience. These tests also aid in ensuring that the system is stable and that changes don't unintentionally interfere with already-existing functionality.

The need for smooth integration to create a fluid experience grows as the web depends more and more on dynamic, data-driven apps. Web apps have evolved from static webpages to highly dynamic platforms that enable real-time activities, including live data tracking, video conferencing, and chat. These apps can manage high user numbers and real-time data transfers without experiencing performance degradation when seamless integration is achieved. One of the best examples of the technologies used to accomplish smooth data flow is WebSockets, which allow real-time communication between the client and server. A messaging app, for example, depends on a continuous connection between the front-end and back-end, requiring that messages submitted by one user be displayed to the recipient right away. Real-time, reliable communication in this situation depends on the server, database, and client-side application all integrating seamlessly.

Furthermore, with full-stack web development, security is still a top priority. Every tier of the technology stack is susceptible to possible security risks, including SQL injection attacks on the back end and cross-site scripting (XSS) flaws on the front end. Implementing security best practices across all stack components requires seamless integration. For example, the application should implement security features like data sanitization, input validation, and authentication methods consistently. This guarantees that sensitive information cannot be accessed by unauthorized users and that any data transferred from the client to the server is secure. Developers can lessen the likelihood that an attack will be successful and safeguard the integrity of the application by keeping security measures consistent throughout the front-end and back-end.

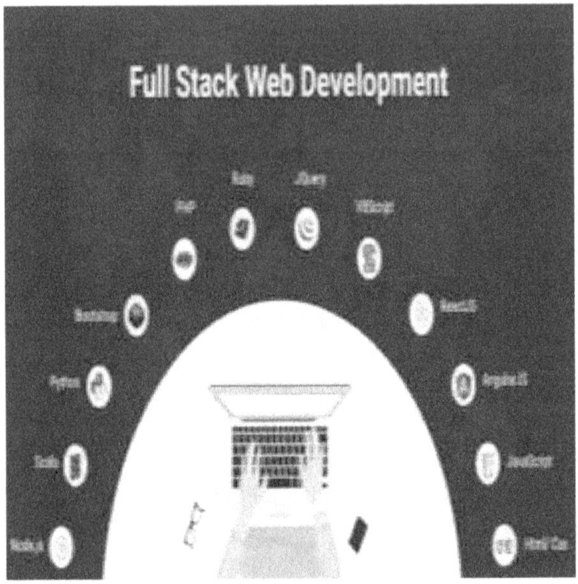

To sum up, the success of every web application depends on smooth integration in full-stack web development. Building effective, fast, and dependable apps requires the integration of all technology stack components, from boosting performance, security, and scalability to increasing user experience. Full-stack engineers will remain essential in ensuring that the front-end and back- end layers function in unison as the web development environment changes. Developers can produce applications that satisfy user needs and set up companies for success in the fiercely competitive digital market by concentrating on seamless integration.

CHAPTER II
Front-End Fundamentals

HTML & CSS Basics

The web's fundamental building components are HTML (HyperText Markup Language) and CSS (Cascading Style Sheets). When combined, they make it possible to create and style web pages. These two technologies are the main tools used in full-stack web development for applying visual design and organizing content. HTML and CSS are the foundation of any web application, regardless of its functionality or level of complexity. These tools are crucial for developing aesthetically pleasing and intuitive user interfaces that communicate with back-end services. Therefore, full-stack developers need to be well-versed in them.

The markup language used to specify a webpage's structure is called HTML. By recognizing components like headings, paragraphs, links, images, and lists, it provides the page's framework. Browsers use tags to mark up certain elements, which they then interpret to show content. HTML concentrates on structuring and meaningfully organizing text rather than presentation or style. In order to identify particular areas of the page, HTML tags are usually nested within one another to form a hierarchy.

A doctype declaration and an initial `<html>` tag are the first two elements of a basic HTML page. The `<head>` and the `<body>` are the two main components that make up the `<html>` element. The page's title, character encoding, and connections to other files, like stylesheets or scripts, are all included in the `<head>` section. The page's actual content, which includes text, graphics, forms, and other user-interactive components, is contained in the `<body>` section.

On the other side, a webpage's presentation can be managed via CSS. While HTML supplies the framework, CSS controls the visual representation of that framework. Developers may manage elements like layout, colors, fonts, spacing, and placement via CSS. It makes the development process more flexible and efficient by enabling the separation of presentation and content. For instance, HTML can be used to arrange the content of a website, while CSS can be used to change the overall appearance and feel of the site without changing the content itself.

Selecting HTML components and adding styles to them is how CSS operates. Styles can be defined in an external stylesheet, inline within an HTML element, or in the document's `<head>` section. Because of its lack of scalability and maintainability, inline styles—which are applied directly to individual elements via the `style` attribute—are typically avoided for larger projects. The HTML document's `<head>` section contains a `<style>` tag that defines internal styles. The most popular approach, though, is to use external stylesheets, which let developers apply styles to multiple web pages from a single file. Developers can guarantee that every page on a website has the same design by attaching an external CSS file to an HTML document.

The concept of selectors is one of the fundamental ideas of CSS. An HTML element that requires styling is the target of a selector. Selectors may be based on characteristics, IDs, classes, or categories of elements. For example, a basic selector may apply a particular font size or color to every `<p>` element on a page. Developers can apply styles to certain items or groups of elements using more sophisticated selectors, such as class and ID selectors. While IDs are unique and ought to be applied to just one element on a page, classes are reusable and can be applied to several items.

Properties are also used by CSS to specify the attributes of particular elements. The appearance of text, layout, and spacing on the page is controlled by properties like `color, font size,` `margin,` and `padding.` A value that describes the behavior of each attribute is linked with it. To modify the color of text, for instance, use the `color` property. Its value can be supplied using RGB values, hexadecimal values, color names, or other formats. In a similar vein, developers may manipulate the size and arrangement of items using properties like `width,` `height,` `display,` and `position.`

The ability of CSS to generate layouts is a key feature. The usage of floats was among the first layout control techniques. Nevertheless, this method had limitations and frequently produced erratic results. More complex layout methods like Flexbox and CSS Grid were established by CSS in response to these constraints. Since its introduction in the early 2010s, Flexbox has allowed developers to design responsive, flexible layouts that adjust to various screen sizes. It makes it easier to align and divide up the space between components inside a container. In contrast, CSS Grid provides a two-dimensional layout technology that enables developers to produce intricate grid-based designs. Both Grid and Flexbox are strong tools for making responsive, contemporary web designs.

One of the most important components of contemporary web development is responsive design. Websites must adapt their appearance and content to fit various screen sizes since consumers visit them from a range of devices, such as desktop computers, tablets, and smartphones. CSS media queries are useful in this situation. Developers can use media queries to apply various styles according to the device's dimensions, resolution, and orientation. A webpage can have distinct layouts for small and large screens using media queries, guaranteeing the best possible user experience across all platforms.

JavaScript is frequently combined with HTML and CSS in full-stack web development to produce dynamic, interactive websites. JavaScript makes functionality and interactivity possible, while HTML supplies the structure, and CSS takes care of the styling. The DOM (Document Object Model), which depicts the structure of an HTML page, may be altered by JavaScript, giving developers the ability to dynamically alter content, update styling, or react to user input. The "front-end stack" or "client-side stack" refers to the HTML, CSS, and JavaScript combination since these technologies work within the user's browser.

Despite being mainly utilized for a web application's front end, HTML and CSS are essential to full-stack development. Full-stack engineers are in charge of a web application's front end and back end. The front end, which was developed using HTML, CSS, and JavaScript, communicates with the back end via Application Programming Interfaces (APIs), which enable data transmission and reception. Business logic, database interactions, and server-side functionality are handled by the back end, which is usually constructed using languages like Python, Ruby, or Node.js. Web applications are powered by a unified system that consists of the front-end and back-end.

Both front-end and back-end programming skills are essential for a well-rounded full-stack developer. Although the front-end is built on HTML and CSS, developers also need to know about front-end frameworks and libraries like React, Angular, or Vue.js. With the use of these tools, developers may create increasingly intricate user interfaces and enhance the user experience in general. Furthermore, back-end frameworks and technologies like

Node.js, Django, and Ruby on Rails, which manage server-side tasks and the interface between the front end and the database, should be familiar to full-stack engineers.

Following the most recent HTML and CSS standards is essential for full-stack developers. The standard is HTML5, which brought several new semantic components such as <header>, <footer>, <article>, and <section>. These components provide the page with greater structure and significance, which improves accessibility and search engine optimization. Developers can improve the page's readability for both users and search engines by using this semantic method to better organize the content. More meaningful content structures are made possible by using HTML5 elements, which is particularly crucial for putting SEO (Search Engine Optimization) tactics into practice. Additionally, HTML5 introduced new APIs and features that are now essential to contemporary online apps, such as local storage, offline functionality, and geolocation.

In contrast, CSS3 has brought forth a number of improvements in web design, including media queries, animations, and transitions. Without using JavaScript, developers can now design more dynamic and captivating user interfaces thanks to these functionalities. Designers and developers may create aesthetically pleasing websites while keeping structure (HTML) and styling (CSS) separate, thanks to CSS3's flexibility and capability. Using CSS3's sophisticated features is crucial for full-stack developers to create slick, contemporary user experiences.

Making sure that the front-end design and back-end functions mesh well is one of the difficulties faced by full-stack engineers. When working with back-end technologies, developers need to make sure that the server or database is dynamically generating the data that is displayed on the website via HTML. Understanding server-side languages and frameworks that communicate with databases, handle requests, and return data for front-end display is necessary for this. While HTML and CSS control how the data is displayed to users, these back-end languages—such as Python (with Flask or Django), Ruby (with Rails), and JavaScript (with Node.js)—manage the logic underlying data processing, authentication, and routing.

JavaScript frequently serves as a link between the back-end (server-side code) and front-end (HTML/CSS), allowing data to be sent and received asynchronously without necessitating a complete page reload. Modern front-end frameworks like React, Angular, or Vue.js, or technologies like AJAX (Asynchronous JavaScript and XML), are used to accomplish this. The smooth interaction of HTML components decorated using CSS with JavaScript methods that request data from the back end is essential for a flawless user experience. RESTful APIs and GraphQL, which enable communication between the client (front-end) and server (back-end), are frequently used for these exchanges.

Additionally, full-stack developers need to think about optimizing performance while creating websites, particularly when working with HTML and CSS. High bounce rates might result from users being immediately turned off by a page that loads slowly. Developers must reduce the amount of HTML and CSS files in order to maximize page load times. This can be accomplished by eliminating superfluous CSS, utilizing methods like minification, which eliminates extraneous characters and spaces from code, and utilizing compression tools that minimize file sizes. To cut down on needless overhead, it's also critical to load only the stylesheets and scripts that are absolutely necessary for each page. Additionally, as these assets have a big impact on page load times, developers should optimize photos, videos, and other media files that make up the page's overall size. Performance improvement requires the use of tools like image compression and lazy loading, which loads images only when they are visible.

Full-stack developers must make sure that the HTML and CSS code they produce is responsive and adjustable to different screen sizes as the demand for mobile-first websites rises. The premise behind the mobile-first design is that websites should be made to function well on mobile devices before being scaled to bigger screen sizes like PCs and tablets. This method relies heavily on CSS media queries, which allow developers to apply various styles according to the device's orientation, screen width, and resolution. On smartphones, for example, a website built using mobile-first principles might have a single column layout; however, as the screen size increases, the layout might change to a multi-column format. This guarantees that irrespective of the device being used, consumers will always have a consistent and optimized experience.

To sum up, the core elements of full-stack web development are HTML and CSS. They give web applications their structural and aesthetic underpinnings, empowering programmers to design intuitive and eye-catching user interfaces. Although the tools and methods used in full-stack development change along with the web, HTML and CSS continue to be essential components of the process. Since these technologies are at the heart of any online application, full-stack developers need to be well-versed in them. Developers may produce dynamic, responsive, and captivating web experiences by combining HTML, CSS, and contemporary development techniques.

JavaScript Essentials

JavaScript is a fundamental language that developers need to be able to learn in order to construct web applications that are dynamic, interactive, and fully functional. It is the cornerstone of full-stack web development. JavaScript, which is one of the fundamental technologies of the web, enables developers to add interactivity, change the Document Object Model (DOM), and manage asynchronous processes in web browsers and on servers. HTML and CSS are also core technologies of the web. JavaScript is an essential component for the development of online applications that are responsive, efficient, and scalable. It can be utilized on the client side (front-end) or the server side (back-end). In order to construct sophisticated online apps that provide users with a seamless experience, full-stack developers make use of JavaScript in conjunction with a wide range of frameworks, libraries, and tools.

When it comes to full-stack development, JavaScript's primary function is to facilitate the presentation of dynamic content and to enable programming interactions. Real-time updates, data validation, animations, and interactive components like forms, buttons, and models are all made possible by JavaScript on the client side of the web page. JavaScript also makes it possible for web pages to come to life. The user experience is significantly improved as a result of its ability to facilitate asynchronous data retrieval and manipulation without necessitating a page reload time. For example, the AJAX (Asynchronous JavaScript and XML) features of JavaScript make it possible for data to be retrieved from a server and shown on the page without disrupting the user's engagement with the website. This is absolutely necessary for web apps that need to have a high level of responsiveness and interaction that they can provide.

Additionally, JavaScript also plays a crucial part in the validation process on the client side. The process of validating a form, for instance, guarantees that the information that users enter is correct and formatted appropriately before it is sent to the server. This eliminates the need for extra processing on the server, which results in an improvement in the performance of online applications. The Document Object Model (DOM) is another way in which JavaScript interacts with HTML elements. This interaction enables developers to dynamically add, remove, and update objects on a webpage. This dynamic behavior contributes to the creation of interfaces that are fluid, responsive, and that respond in real-time to the activities of the user.

When it comes to full-stack development, JavaScript is utilized not just on the client side but also on the server side to a significant degree. As a result of its capacity to execute JavaScript on the server, the runtime environment known as Node.js, which is built on JavaScript, has garnered an enormous amount of popularity. Full-stack developers are able to work with the same language throughout both the client and server sides of an application because this reduces the need for developers to use numerous languages for different areas of an application. Node.js is a programming language that utilizes an event-driven, non-blocking input/output mechanism. This makes it particularly well-suited for managing concurrent requests in real-time. In order to construct scalable online applications, this functionality is absolutely necessary. This is especially true for applications that require high performance, such as live-streaming platforms or real-time chat services.

The introduction of Node.js has made it easier to construct frameworks and libraries that are based on JavaScript. One example of this is Express.js, which simplifies server-side development by offering a comprehensive collection of tools for managing routing, middleware, and HTTP requests. Express.js makes the process of developing server-side applications more efficient by minimizing the amount of boilerplate code that is required which increases the amount of time that is spent on development. Node.js and Express.js are two of the technologies that full-stack developers can use in conjunction with other technologies, such as MongoDB, which is a NoSQL database, to handle and store data in a manner that is both flexible and scalable. Through the utilization of JavaScript Object Notation (JSON), MongoDB is able to interface with JavaScript in a smooth manner, which enables efficient data retrieval and manipulation.

In addition, JavaScript is an essential component in the development of Application Programming Interfaces (APIs), which are designed to simplify communication between various components of an application or between apps. JavaScript is typically used to construct RESTful application programming interfaces (APIs), which interact with data by utilizing HTTP methods (GET, POST, PUT, and DELETE). JavaScript is utilized by full-stack developers in order to construct endpoints that are capable of handling requests and returning responses, which are often in the JSON format. This makes it possible for the front end of an application to retrieve data from the back end without having to reload the page, which improves the user experience as a whole. GraphQL is a relatively new query language for application programming interfaces (APIs), and it is frequently used by full-stack developers in conjunction with JavaScript to retrieve data in a more efficient manner. This is accomplished by defining the specific data that is required in a single request.

JavaScript also communicates with third-party services using application programming interfaces (APIs) on the client side, which enables the integration of data and functionality from the outside world. In order to ensure the safety of financial transactions, a full-stack developer can, for instance, incorporate a payment gateway application programming interface (API) like Stripe or PayPal into a web application. In a similar manner, in order to enable social logins, share buttons, and other social features, JavaScript is utilized to connect social media application programming interfaces (APIs) such as Facebook, Twitter, or Google.

The application of JavaScript is not limited to the building of conventional online apps; it is also the foundation of mobile application development, which is accomplished through frameworks such as React Native. Using JavaScript and React, developers are able to construct mobile applications with the help of React Native. This makes it possible for developers to create cross-platform applications that are compatible with both iOS and Android. As a result, the process of developing mobile applications is simplified because it is no longer necessary to acquire knowledge of platform-specific languages like Swift for iOS or Java for Android. Full-stack developers are able to construct applications that are compatible with different platforms by utilizing JavaScript and React Native. These applications make use of a single codebase.

Additionally, JavaScript frameworks and libraries, such as React, Angular, and Vue.js, have simplified the process of designing dynamic, component-based user interfaces, which has further contributed to the revolution in front-end development. The user interface (UI) can be broken down into reusable components with the help of these frameworks, which makes the development process more modular, thereby increasing its efficiency and maintaining its maintainability. A declarative method is utilized by React, for instance, in order to construct user interfaces. This approach allows developers to define the appearance of the user interface based on the current state of the application. This reduces the need for manual manipulation of the Document Object Model (DOM) and streamlines the process of updating the user interface

(UI) whenever the state of the application changes. React's virtual DOM also increases performance by reducing the amount of updates that are necessary to render changes to the actual DOM. This results in faster rendering times, which in turn speeds up the rendering process.

Angular, which is a comprehensive framework built by Google, offers a comprehensive solution for the construction of single-page applications (SPAs). A strong routing system, two-way data binding, and dependency injection are some of the elements that are included in its comprehensive collection of tools for the development of data-driven, dynamic web applications. The provision of a structured framework that assists in the organization of the code and the maintenance of scalability is one of the reasons why Angular is particularly useful for the construction of large-scale applications that have complicated user interfaces. Vue.js is yet another well-known front-end framework that is renowned for its ease of use and capacity for adaptability. It gives developers the ability to gradually embrace the framework by integrating it with projects that are already in existence or by using it to construct full-scale applications that are single-page in nature.

When it comes to full-stack web development, having a solid understanding of JavaScript and the ecosystem of frameworks, libraries, and tools that go along with it is absolutely necessary for the construction of cutting-edge, high-performance web apps. As the JavaScript programming language continues to undergo development, with frequent revisions to its syntax, features, and best practices, it is imperative that developers remain current with the most recent improvements. The introduction of technologies such as ES6 (ECMAScript 2015) has resulted in enhancements to the language. These additions include arrow functions, classes, template literals, destructuring, and async/await, all of which improve the readability, maintainability, and efficiency of code written in JavaScript. Full-stack engineers are required to have a strong understanding of these newly introduced capabilities in order to guarantee that the code they write is clean, efficient, and up-to-date.

JavaScript developers, in addition to working with the language itself, also collaborate with a variety of build tools, package managers, and version control systems in order to speed the development process. It is possible for developers to bundle and transpile their code with the use of tools such as Webpack, Babel, and Parcel. This ensures that the code is able to run effectively across a variety of browsers and contexts. It is possible for developers to manage dependencies with the use of package managers like npm (Node Package Manager) and Yarn. This allows them to be certain that their projects are utilizing the appropriate versions of libraries and packages. The use of version control systems such as Git gives developers the ability to monitor changes made to their code, work together with other members of their team, and release their applications with complete assurance.

As a result of the fact that full-stack development encompasses both front-end and back-end components, JavaScript serves as the adhesive that binds these two regions of an application together. One of the most important aspects of full-stack development is the integration of JavaScript with databases. This is especially true when working with NoSQL databases such as MongoDB, which store data in a format that is compatible with JavaScript objects. JavaScript is utilized by full-stack developers in order to communicate with the database, retrieve data, and then transmit it to the front end for display. In addition, they make use of JavaScript to manage CRUD activities, which stands for create, read, update, and delete. This helps to ensure that data is managed effectively across the program.

Due to the fact that it is used to power both the client-side and the server side of web development, JavaScript is an essential ability for full-stack developers to possess. JavaScript is a powerful programming language that enables developers to construct online applications that are dynamic, scalable, and high-performing. It may be used for a variety of purposes, including the creation of interactive user interfaces and the management of asynchronous requests. In order to be successful in the construction of contemporary online applications, full-stack developers need to have a strong command of JavaScript, in addition to the frameworks, libraries, and tools that are designed to support it. JavaScript continues to be an essential technology that every full-stack developer needs to be proficient in, despite the fact that the web development landscape is always shifting.

Front-End Frameworks

Front-end frameworks serve as the basis for developing user interfaces and the general organization of a web application, making them indispensable tools in contemporary web development. By providing standardized structures, reusable components, and development-streamlining tools, these frameworks enable developers to create dynamic, quick, and efficient websites and applications. Front-end frameworks have grown to be an essential component of full-stack web development over time, allowing developers to concentrate less on creating the wheel and more on business logic. From creating the user interface to managing data interactions and making sure the application functions properly across various devices and browsers, these frameworks provide libraries, tools, and conventions that assist in managing a variety of tasks in web development.

The increasing complexity of contemporary web applications has fueled the development of front-end frameworks. In the early days of web development, developers manually coded every component of a website or application using static HTML, CSS, and JavaScript. However, the need for more potent tools to handle intricate front-end workflows increased along with user expectations for interactive, responsive, and aesthetically pleasing web experiences. This issue was addressed by front-end frameworks, which provide pre-made elements, responsive layouts, and tools for creating complex user experiences without having to start from scratch.

The time that a front-end framework saves developers is one of its main benefits. Without having to individually code each component, developers may easily construct complicated interfaces using a set of pre-configured components and layouts. This facilitates quicker iteration, guarantees consistency throughout the application, and lessens redundancy. To further expedite the development process, frameworks frequently come with pre-configured build tools that automate processes like minification, bundling, and transpiring.

Vue.js, Angular, and React are some of the most popular front-end frameworks. All of these frameworks are made to assist developers in creating cutting-edge, dynamic web applications, but each has its own special features, advantages, and learning curves. Facebook created the well-known framework React, which is renowned for its component-based design. Individual components, which are reusable bits of code that manage particular interface elements, are used to construct the user interface in React. Better code organization is made possible by this modular approach, which also facilitates application maintenance and updates.

The virtual DOM, a fundamental component of React, streamlines the user interface rendering process. Every time a change is made, React generates a virtual DOM in memory and compares it to the prior version rather than immediately altering the real DOM. Performance and user experience are enhanced as a result of the differences being efficiently updated in the actual DOM. Because of its great flexibility, developers may combine React with a wide range of other tools and libraries, such as React Router for navigation and Redux for state management.

Another well-known front-end framework that has a more subjective approach to application development is Angular, which was created by Google. A complete collection of tools for creating single-page applications (SPAs) is offered by the Angular framework. Angular is a comprehensive solution that contains tools for routing, state management, form handling, and dependency injection, in contrast to React, which largely concentrates on the view layer. The foundation of Angular is the idea of components and services, where the former is in charge of the view, and the latter is in charge of data operations and business logic.

Angular's two-way data binding, which enables automated synchronization between the model and the view, is one of its most notable features. The view automatically updates as the model (data) does, and vice versa. This guarantees that the user interface is constantly in sync with the underlying data and lessens the need for manual DOM manipulation. Additionally, Angular comes with a robust templating system that lets developers utilize HTML to declaratively describe the user interface's structure while including Angular-specific directives and expressions to include dynamic content and logic.

Another well-liked front-end framework is Vue.js, which is renowned for being straightforward and simple to integrate. Because it may be implemented gradually, Vue.js is frequently referred to as a progressive framework. Using Vue.js, developers may begin by adding interactivity to a tiny portion of a website and work their way up to a complete application. Although Vue.js and React both employ component-based architecture, Vue.js is less opinionated, allowing developers greater freedom in how they organize their apps.

Vue.js's reactivity system, which dynamically adjusts the user interface when the underlying data changes, is one of its primary characteristics. Similar to Angular, Vue.js offers a versatile templating vocabulary that lets programmers specify the layout of their user interface while incorporating logic using directives unique to Vue. Compared to Angular, Vue.js has a comparatively flat learning curve, which makes it an excellent option for developers who are unfamiliar with front-end frameworks or who need to create tiny applications fast.

There are a number of additional front-end frameworks and libraries that provide special functionality and address particular use cases in addition to React, Angular, and Vue.js. Svelte, for instance, is a more recent framework that differs from more established ones like Angular and React. Svelte combines components into highly optimized JavaScript code during the build process, in contrast to other frameworks that employ a virtual DOM and update the real DOM during runtime. Performance is accelerated by doing away with the requirement for a virtual DOM and lowering the overhead related to rendering UI modifications.

Ember.js is another noteworthy framework that is well-known for its strong convention-over-configuration stance. Because Ember.js offers a collection of pre-established patterns and conventions for application structuring, developers may get started more quickly and with fewer architectural choices. Ember.js is perfect for creating intricate applications with lots of interactivity because it also has a strong router and state management mechanism.

Additionally, there are front-end frameworks specifically designed for creating mobile applications. For instance, React Native enables developers to use React to create cross-platform mobile applications. Similar to those found in React, React Native offers a collection of components that are mobile-friendly. This saves time and effort by enabling developers to create code only once and have it run on both iOS and Android. Tools for developing mobile applications with web technologies are also offered by other frameworks, such as Ionic and NativeScript.

Although front-end frameworks have many benefits, there are drawbacks as well. The high learning curve of front-end frameworks is one of its primary critiques; this is especially true for frameworks like Angular and React, which demand that developers acquire new ideas like components, state management, and routing. Furthermore, developers need to continuously stay current with the newest tools, libraries, and best practices due to the rapid evolution of the front-end development landscape. For novices or developers who are already overseeing several projects, this could be too much to handle.

The performance presents another difficulty. Even while front-end frameworks like Angular and React are meant to be efficient, improper use can still cause performance problems. Inadequately optimized components, for instance, may result in needless re-renders, which can slow down page loads and negatively impact user experience. For their apps to function successfully, developers need to be aware of best practices like code splitting, lazy loading, and memoization.

Notwithstanding these difficulties, front-end frameworks have transformed web development by simplifying the creation of scalable, responsive, and dynamic web applications. These frameworks provide quicker development cycles, better code quality, and a more efficient method of creating intricate user interfaces by giving developers pre-built components, tools, and conventions. Front-end frameworks are now a crucial component of the contemporary web development toolset, regardless of the complexity of the single-page application or the website you're creating.

A key idea in contemporary front-end programming is state management, particularly when working on intricate systems that call for communication between numerous components and the server. The user interface of single-page applications (SPAs) is frequently dynamic, with numerous page elements changing in response to user input or data modifications. This calls for an effective method of controlling and coordinating the state of the application; state management solutions in front-end frameworks are useful for this.

The administration of the data that powers the application's user interface is referred to as state management in frameworks such as React. Each component in React has its own state that can be altered in reaction to user input or other events because the state is local to the component. However, as the program gets bigger, component-level state management can become more difficult, making it harder to share data between components. Developers can use libraries like Redux, Context API, or MobX, which offer a centralized method of managing the state throughout the entire program, to solve this problem.

By centralizing the information in a store, Redux, one of the most popular state management frameworks in the React ecosystem, enables developers to manage the state in a predictable manner. Reducers control how the state is updated, and actions are sent out to update it. Even in huge and complicated applications, this architecture guarantees that the data flow of the application stays transparent and consistent. Redux has several benefits, like consistent application state and easier debugging, despite its often high learning curve.

In contrast, Angular's dependency injection architecture and services provide an integrated state management solution. Angular services facilitate data sharing across components by managing shared state and business logic. NgRx, a Redux-inspired utility that provides a more systematic approach to state management for larger apps, is another tool included with Angular. NgRx manages the state of the application in a reactive manner by utilizing the store architecture and integrating ideas such as actions, reducers, and effects.

Vuex is the state management library offered by Vue.js. However it is also capable of maintaining the state within individual components. Similar to Redux, Vuex uses a centralized store to store the state of the application and offers mutations and actions to update it. Developers can easily handle state changes and make sure the user interface is always in sync with the data, thanks to Vuex's smooth integration with Vue's reactivity system. In order to improve maintainability, developers can divide the state management logic into several files using Vuex's module support.

To sum up, front-end frameworks are essential to contemporary web development because they give programmers the structure and tools they need to create user interfaces that are quick, interactive, and maintainable. Frameworks like React, Angular, Vue.js, and others have established themselves as industry standards, giving programmers strong tools to handle the challenges of creating dynamic websites. Although these frameworks present a unique set of difficulties, full-stack developers find them invaluable due to the advantages they offer in terms of speed, efficiency, and maintainability. Front-end frameworks will continue to be an essential component of the development ecosystem as the web develops further, assisting developers in producing smooth and captivating user experiences.

CHAPTER III
Back-End Foundations

Server-Side Programming

Server-side programming plays a crucial role in full-stack web development, where it is responsible for handling the back-end processes and ensuring the efficient functioning of web applications. Server-side programming is focused on controlling data, logic, and communication between the client and the server, as opposed to client-side programming, which concentrates on what the user sees and interacts with within the browser. Although it is frequently concealed from the user, this part of web development is essential to producing powerful, dynamic, and interactive apps.

Database creation and administration, application logic, authorization and authentication procedures, and system-to-system communication are all typically included in server-side programming. There is a wide range of programming languages and frameworks available for server-side development, and the selection of technology is influenced by the needs of the project, developer experience, and scalability. Python, Ruby, PHP, C#, JavaScript (Node.js), and Java are popular server-side languages. Although each of these languages has advantages and disadvantages of its own, they are frequently combined with frameworks and libraries that facilitate development and offer strong instruments for creating systems that are scalable and maintainable.

JavaScript can now be utilized on the server side thanks to Node.js, which has grown in popularity recently, especially among developers who are already familiar with JavaScript. Because of its speedy and lightweight event-driven, non-blocking I/O approach, Node.js is a good choice for developing real-time applications such as chat apps and collaborative platforms. Libraries like Express.js, which are abundant in the Node.js environment, make it easier to handle middleware, route requests, and communicate with databases. Specifically, Express.js is a simple web framework for Node.js that provides an adaptable and effective method for managing HTTP requests and responses. Because Node.js is asynchronous and non-blocking, developers may create scalable apps that manage several concurrent connections with no overhead.

Another well-liked option for server-side programming is Python, particularly for programmers involved in data science, machine learning, and artificial intelligence. Python is a great option for quick development because of its well-known readability, simplicity, and extensive standard library. The two Python web frameworks that are most frequently used are Django and Flask. As a high-level framework that adheres to the "batteries-included" idea, Django has a number of built-in utilities that greatly expedite the development process, including form handling, database administration, and authentication. Contrarily, Flask is a lightweight micro-framework that allows developers greater flexibility over the way their applications are constructed, which makes it appropriate for smaller projects or developers who would like to work more directly.

Ruby on Rails, or just Rails, is a Ruby-based framework for server-side web applications. The convention over configuration (CoC) and don't repeat yourself (DRY) principles, which Rails adheres to, enable programmers to create code that is clear, effective, and maintainable. Because of its pre-configured options that make many routine jobs easier and its emphasis on automation, Rails is renowned for being developer-friendly. Rails is a great option for developers who want to create web apps fast because it comes with built-in features for managing database migrations, user authentication, and session management. Notwithstanding its benefits, Rails has drawn criticism for being overly sentimental, which in certain situations restricts adaptability.

PHP is still a major participant in server-side programming despite being frequently seen as an obsolete technology. It continues to be widely used in the web development business and underpins numerous content management systems, including WordPress. The Laravel framework, which offers a cutting-edge, sophisticated toolbox for creating online applications, is frequently used in conjunction with PHP. With its many features, like built-in routing, authentication, and database migrations, Laravel makes it simpler for developers to get started. PHP remains one of the most popular languages for server-side programming because of its scalability, ease of use, and abundance of resources, even in spite of complaints about its inconsistent syntax and previous security flaws.

Java is a well-known programming language that is favored for large-scale systems and enterprise-level applications. Java is renowned for its cross-platform interoperability, scalability, and dependability. With the Spring framework, which offers an extensive collection of tools for creating safe, scalable, and stable online applications, it is frequently utilized in server-side development. Enterprise application development is made easier with the support of the Spring framework's many components, which include Spring Boot, Spring Data, and Spring Security. Java is a great option for mission-critical applications that require high performance and dependability because of its robust typing and extensive ecosystem of libraries and tools.

In server-side web development, C# and the.NET framework are also frequently utilized, especially for applications that run in Microsoft settings. Part of the broader.NET ecosystem, which consists of a collection of tools and frameworks for creating desktop, mobile, and web applications, is the object-oriented programming language C#. The main web framework for creating server-side C# applications is called ASP.NET. Because of its great performance, security, and smooth integration with the rest of the Microsoft stack, developers at businesses that depend on Microsoft technology favor it.

The administration of databases, which are used to store and retrieve data for online applications, is one of the most crucial components of server-side development. Server-side developers need to be well-versed in data integrity, query optimization, and database design. Relational databases and NoSQL databases are the two main database types used in server-side programming. Structured tables with preset schemas are used to store data in relational databases like Microsoft SQL Server, PostgreSQL, and MySQL. Applications like content management systems, financial apps, and e-commerce platforms that need sophisticated queries and data linkages benefit greatly from these databases. When working with relational databases, developers create queries using SQL (Structured Query Language) to retrieve, insert, update, and delete data.

However, NoSQL databases—like MongoDB, CouchDB, and Cassandra—are made to work with semi-structured or unstructured data. Because of their great scalability and flexibility, NoSQL databases are perfect for applications that need to store a lot of data in a variety of forms. For instance, real-time analytics, social networking platforms, and applications with a lot of user-generated content frequently use NoSQL databases. Developers can store data in formats like JSON, BSON, or XML in these databases, which do not rely on set schemas. NoSQL databases' scalability and flexibility make them appropriate for contemporary applications with changing data needs.

Along with database administration, server-side programming entails developing and managing the business logic that controls the application's data processing and manipulation. Writing code to manage user sessions, process payments, issue notifications, handle user authentication and authorization, and communicate with third-party APIs are all included in this. Server-side logic is in charge of making sure that users engage with the program in meaningful ways and that data is processed securely and effectively. When a user signs into an application, for example, the server-side code establishes a session, confirms the user's credentials, and provides the client with the relevant answer.

Implementing API (Application development Interface) endpoints, which facilitate communication between the server and the client as well as with other systems, is another crucial component of server-side development. Full-stack web development frequently uses REST (Representational State Transfer) APIs because they enable clients to send HTTP requests to the server for tasks like creating, reading, updating, or removing data. In order to handle requests accurately and provide pertinent results in a timely manner, server-side developers must provide APIs that are safe, effective, and simple to use.

Additionally, server-side programming is in charge of guaranteeing the security of the online application and the protection of user data. To avoid security flaws like SQL injection, cross-site scripting (XSS), and cross-site request forgery (CSRF), this entails putting in place security measures, including data encryption, secure authentication, and input validation. In order to ensure that their applications adhere to the necessary legal and ethical standards for data privacy and protection, server-side developers must also be aware of compliance regulations, such as the General Data Protection Regulation (GDPR) in the European Union.

Ensuring scalability and performance is a challenge in server-side development, particularly when online applications get more complex and have more users. Applications created by server-side developers need to be built to withstand large traffic volumes and effectively handle requests. This could entail employing load balancing to divide traffic among several servers, optimizing database queries, utilizing cloud-based services that can automatically scale in response to demand, and utilizing caching techniques to store frequently accessed data. Developers may simplify the deployment process and manage server-side infrastructure with the use of tools like Docker and Kubernetes.

DevOps techniques, which emphasize automating the creation, testing, and deployment of online applications, are also strongly related to server-side programming. Pipelines for continuous integration (CI) and continuous delivery (CD) are frequently used to guarantee that server-side code is automatically tested, constructed, and deployed. This lowers the possibility of errors and enhances the development process overall by ensuring that application updates are implemented promptly and consistently.

Additionally, load balancing is essential for performance. In applications with a lot of traffic, the server may soon be overloaded with requests. Load balancing facilitates the equitable distribution of incoming traffic among several servers or application instances. Preventing any one server from becoming overloaded lowers the possibility of server failure or sluggish response times. A reverse proxy, specific hardware devices, or the DNS level are some of the application layers where load balancing can be used. In order to handle growing traffic needs, load balancing is sometimes combined with horizontal scaling, which entails adding more servers to the system. In contrast, vertical scaling is the process of adding extra CPU or RAM to a single server in order to increase its computing capacity. For web applications to be resilient and scalable, both scaling strategies are necessary.

Another key issue with server-side programming is data consistency and dependability. Web applications frequently have to manage massive volumes of user data, transactions, and other crucial business processes as they expand. It is essential to make sure that this data is correct and consistent throughout the system. Applications like banking systems and e-commerce platforms that need fault tolerance and high availability should pay particular attention to this. It might be difficult to achieve data consistency in distributed systems. The CAP theorem, which describes the trade-offs between consistency, availability, and partition tolerance, is one way to solve the problem. A distributed system cannot concurrently guarantee all three qualities, according to the CAP theorem. Rather, the application's needs force developers to make a trade-off. For instance, a system might give priority to consistency in applications that manage crucial financial transactions or to availability when users require constant access to the system.

Security is a persistent issue in server-side development that necessitates continuous attention to detail. A web application's back end must be protected in order to protect user data, stop illegal access, and guarantee that the application works as intended. Putting in place appropriate authorization and authentication procedures is one of the core steps in web application security. While authorization establishes the user's access permissions within the application, authentication confirms a user's identity, usually utilizing credentials like usernames and passwords. Multi-factor authentication (MFA), which requires users to submit extra proof of identity beyond a password, such as a one-time code texted to their phone or an authenticator app, is a popular security strategy for authentication. Role-based access control (RBAC), in which several user roles are given distinct rights within the application, is a popular technique used by developers for authorization. For instance, an administrator has complete authority over the system, whereas a regular user may only be able to read specific items.

Conclusively, server-side programming is an essential component of full-stack web development, handling application logic, data management, and facilitating seamless client-server communication. Server-side developers build safe, scalable, and effective online apps using a range of languages, frameworks, and technologies. Server-side programming will continue to be essential to creating cutting-edge, dynamic online applications that satisfy the needs of both consumers and companies as web development advances. In order to shape the user experience and guarantee the success of online applications, server-side programming is essential due to its emphasis on data management, application logic, security, and performance.

Database Management

In essence, a database is an organized set of data that makes effective storage and retrieval possible. The database is in charge of preserving the data's integrity and making sure that it is accessible for a variety of actions, including inserts, deletions, updates, and queries. A web application's performance, scalability, and security are all directly impacted by efficient database management. A well-managed and structured database can handle complicated data operations, guarantee data consistency, and enhance the user experience overall.

Relational databases and non-relational databases are the two main database formats that are frequently utilized in full-stack web development. Data is stored in tables that are connected by relationships in relational databases like MySQL, PostgreSQL, and SQLite. These connections make it possible to organize data in a way that guarantees data integrity and minimizes redundancy. MongoDB, CouchDB, and Cassandra are examples of non-relational databases, or NoSQL databases, which store data in more adaptable formats such as key-value pairs or JSON. These databases are usually employed where flexibility, speed, and scalability are more crucial than rigorous data consistency.

Relational databases are especially helpful in situations where the relationships between data elements are important and the data is structured and necessitates sophisticated querying. To guarantee that the system runs effectively, for instance, the interactions between consumers, orders, items, and inventories must be carefully maintained in an e-commerce platform. With foreign keys connecting tables, a relational database's tables are arranged to reflect these relationships. This enables developers to run intricate SQL queries that have multiple ways to retrieve, alter, and aggregate data. The standard programming language for interacting with relational databases is called SQL (Structured Query Language), which enables programmers to create queries that can execute actions on big datasets or retrieve particular data.

The capacity of relational databases to enforce data integrity through the use of features like constraints, primary keys, and foreign keys is one of their main advantages. Each entry in a table is uniquely identified by its primary key, which guarantees that each record is unique and accessible by other tables. Conversely, foreign keys are used to create connections across tables so that data in one table can be referred to in another. By guaranteeing the validity of the references between tables, this helps preserve the data's consistency. To make sure that the data complies with specified requirements, like a field not being left empty or a value being within a given range, constraints like not null, unique, and check are employed.

On the other hand, non-relational databases are frequently chosen when the system must scale horizontally over several servers or when the data is unstructured or semi-structured. Scaling out and adapting to changes in the data model is made easier by the more flexible structure in which data is stored in non-relational databases. Users on a social networking site, for instance, might have a variety of content, including text postings, photos, and videos, and their connections with other users—like friends or followers—may evolve over time. This type of adaptable, changing data structure works better with a non-relational database since it doesn't need a preset schema. As a result, developers can modify the data model or add new data types without having to completely rebuild the database. Furthermore, NoSQL databases are easier to scale than conventional relational databases, which makes them ideal for managing substantial volumes of unstructured data, including log data or user-generated content.

The capacity of non-relational databases to scale horizontally is one of their main benefits. Instead of improving the hardware of a single computer, horizontal scaling allows for the addition of additional machines or instances to manage rising load. In contemporary web applications that must divide the burden among several servers due to excessive traffic, this can be especially helpful. Non-relational databases, such as MongoDB and Cassandra, manage data replication and distribution automatically and are built to expand across numerous nodes. This makes them perfect for applications like real-time apps, big data apps, and mobile apps that need to be highly available and able to manage huge traffic volumes.

Non-relational databases have trade-offs even though they are flexible and scalable. The fact that NoSQL databases frequently do not provide the same degree of data consistency as relational databases is one of their primary drawbacks. Specifically, a lot of NoSQL databases use the "eventual consistency" concept, which means that changes made to the database could take a while to reach every node in a distributed system. Temporary data inconsistencies may result from this, which could be problematic in some applications where accuracy and consistency are crucial, like financial systems. Some NoSQL databases have options that offer tighter consistency guarantees in order to address this; however, doing so may result in decreased speed or scalability.

Building dependable, scalable, and effective applications in full-stack development requires knowing whether to employ relational versus non-relational databases. Relational databases are frequently a preferable option for applications with intricate data relationships and stringent consistency requirements. Non-relational databases, on the other hand, can be better suitable for applications that need to manage substantial volumes of unstructured data or that demand great scalability. The type of data being kept, the need for flexibility, the size of the application, and the particular performance needs all play a role in the decision between relational and non-relational databases.

Choosing the correct database is only one aspect of database management in full-stack development. Another important factor that greatly influences a web application's effectiveness is an efficient database design. Creating tables and the links between them, establishing the database's structure, and making sure the data is arranged to facilitate effective searches and updates are all part of database design. Normalization, which entails arranging data to reduce redundancy and make sure the database is designed to facilitate effective data retrieval, is one of the fundamental concepts of database design. The process of normalization is dividing big, complicated tables into smaller, easier-to-manage tables, each of which contains information pertaining to a distinct item or idea. This guarantees continuous and trustworthy data updates and helps avoid data abnormalities.

Nevertheless, even though normalization is a crucial component of database architecture, there are circumstances in which denormalizing the database might be required. In order to increase performance, denormalization is purposefully adding redundancy to the database, usually by lowering the number of joins needed in queries. Applications that need quick read operations and where the performance overhead of combining several tables is too high may find this especially helpful. Denormalization can speed up searches by simplifying database joins in situations where read performance is crucial, but it comes at the expense of some data redundancy and the possibility of data inconsistencies.

Another crucial component of database administration is database indexing. By building a data structure that enables quicker lookups of particular values within a table, indexes are used to speed up data retrieval. In the absence of indexes, database queries would have to go through each record in a table to locate the pertinent information, which can be time-consuming, particularly when dealing with big datasets. Developers can greatly enhance the efficiency of specific queries by building indexes on frequently searched columns. Nevertheless, there are drawbacks to indexes, as they may cause writing operations like inserts, updates, and deletions to lag. Therefore, depending on the kinds of queries that will be run most frequently, it is crucial to carefully determine which columns to index.

Data integrity is another crucial component of database administration. The quality, consistency, and dependability of the data kept in the database are referred to as data integrity. Because corrupted or inconsistent data can result in mistakes, erroneous results, and broken functionality in web applications, it is imperative to ensure data integrity. Using constraints, such as primary keys, foreign keys, and unique constraints, is one of the fundamental strategies to preserve data integrity. While foreign keys guarantee consistent associations between tables, primary keys guarantee that every entry in a table is unique. Developers can also enforce business logic and guarantee that data is entered into the database accurately by using validation rules and triggers.

Disaster recovery and backups are also crucial components of database administration. In the case of hardware failure, data corruption, or other calamities, a solid backup plan guarantees that data can be recovered. To prevent data loss, regular backups should be made and kept in a secure location, like a cloud storage service or an offsite server. Developers should also put disaster recovery plans into practice, which specify how to restore the database and application in the event of an emergency. This may entail testing the recovery procedure to make sure it functions when required and configuring replication and clustering to provide high availability.

Lastly, database performance tuning is a continual procedure that entails tracking and improving database performance as the application expands. To increase performance, this entails examining sluggish queries, locating bottlenecks, and modifying the database schema, queries, or indexes. Profiling tools and performance monitoring software are frequently used by database administrators (DBAs) to find areas for improvement and make sure the database can manage growing traffic and data quantities.

A crucial component of full-stack web development, database administration affects an online application's overall performance, scalability, and dependability. Developers must be able to comprehend the many kinds of databases, create effective database schemas, and use best practices for data management. Developers may make sure that the backend of their web application runs smoothly and securely by carefully choosing the best database for the application's requirements, guaranteeing data integrity, maximizing performance, and making backup and disaster recovery plans.

To sum up, database administration is essential to full-stack web development because it makes sure that data is effectively structured, saved, and made available. Developers must carefully select the best database solution based on the particular requirements of the application, whether they choose a relational database, which prioritizes structured data and complex relationships, or a non-relational database, which provides flexibility and scalability for unstructured data. Good database architecture is essential for seamless application performance since it helps avoid redundancy and guarantees data consistency through normalization, indexing, and data integrity management.

Authentication & Security

Security and authentication are essential components of any full-stack web development project. Ensuring the security of user data and the integrity of the overall application is crucial as web apps grow increasingly intricate and interface with multiple platforms and services. Devastating outcomes, such as unauthorized access to private data, data loss, and reputational harm, might result from a security breach or an error in authentication procedures. As a result, developers working on full-stack applications must comprehend the foundations of authentication and the different security methods.

The process of confirming a user's or system's identification is important to authentication. Making sure that only authorized users may access particular areas of the program is the first step in securing any online application. Many techniques, including passwords, biometrics, two-factor authentication (2FA), and OAuth, are commonly used to accomplish authentication. Passwords are the most widely used authentication method among these, but their vulnerability to attacks like brute force and credential stuffing is making them appear less safe. Because of this, more reliable authentication methods are frequently used in contemporary applications.

Because it adds an extra degree of protection beyond passwords, two-factor authentication (2FA) has become a standard practice in web development. Users are required to supply two means of identification when using 2FA, typically a mobile phone or authentication app and something they know, like a password. Even if an attacker manages to get the password, this greatly lowers the likelihood that they will be able to access an account without authorization.

OAuth is another widely used authentication technique in full-stack development that enables users to provide resources to third-party apps without disclosing their passwords. Applications are frequently integrated with well-known services like Google, Facebook, and GitHub using OAuth. For example, a user can use their Google login information to access a web service, which simplifies the login procedure and removes the need to memorize a different password.

Authorization establishes what an authenticated user is permitted to perform within the program, whereas authentication confirms a user's identity. This entails controlling access control and making sure users can only access the information or features that they are allowed to. Users are given roles under the popular authorization model known as role-based access control (RBAC), and each position has particular rights attached to it. For instance, a typical user may only have access to specific functionalities, but an administrator may have access to every aspect of the system. To make sure that users cannot access restricted resources without authorization, it is essential to implement appropriate access controls and verify user permissions at every application layer.

Securing the data that passes through online applications must be a top priority for developers, in addition to user authentication and authorization. Particularly in full-stack web development, where sensitive data and user input must be handled by both the front end and the back end, data security is a major challenge. Problems, including data loss, tampering, and theft, may result from a data security breach. Encryption is frequently used to safeguard data while it is in transit and at rest in order to avoid such accidents.

Secure protocols like HTTPS and SSL/TLS are used to encrypt client-server communication for data in transit. This guarantees that hackers cannot intercept any sensitive data while it is being transmitted, including login credentials or personal information. In order to create a secure connection between the browser and the server and enable safe data transfer, SSL/TLS certificates are necessary.

Similarly, encryption is crucial for data that is at rest. Developers should utilize encryption methods like AES (Advanced Encryption Standard) when storing sensitive data in a database or file system to guarantee that the data is safe even in the event that an attacker manages to access the server. Furthermore, it is essential to protect the encryption keys since compromised keys can make the encryption ineffective. Encryption solutions for data at rest are available from numerous cloud providers and hosting platforms, and they can be set up during database setup.

Defending against common web vulnerabilities is another crucial component of security in full-stack web development. The major security threats for online applications, such as injection attacks, cross-site scripting (XSS), cross-site request forgery (CSRF), and security misconfigurations, are listed in detail by the Open Online Application Security Project (OWASP). Developers must take proactive steps to protect against these vulnerabilities, as each one might expose an application to different types of attacks.

One of the most prevalent and harmful flaws in online applications is SQL injection. By inserting malicious code into an input field, an attacker can manipulate an SQL query and possibly gain access to or change the database. Because prepared statements or parameterized queries isolate the query structure from user input, malicious input cannot change the query's behavior, which is why developers should always use them to prevent SQL injection.

Attacks such as cross-site scripting (XSS) entail inserting harmful code into websites that other users are viewing. These scripts have the ability to deface pages, steal session cookies, and send users to harmful websites. Developers must encode or escape special characters that can be regarded as code in order to sanitize user inputs and prevent cross-site scripting attacks. By limiting the sources from which scripts can be loaded, security headers like Content Security Policy (CSP) can also help reduce the danger of XSS attacks.

Attacks such as cross-site request forgery (CSRF) entail deceiving a legitimate user into carrying out unwanted operations on an online application. An attacker might, for instance, create a fraudulent link or form that, when clicked, causes the victim's account to change or have money transferred. Developers can utilize anti-CSRF tokens, which are distinct tokens provided in requests that must match the token saved on the server to stop CSRF attacks. The request is denied if the tokens do not match.

When developers neglect to appropriately set up their server or web application settings, security misconfigurations may arise, leaving vulnerabilities vulnerable to exploitation. This includes failing to deploy security patches, keeping default configurations in place, or revealing private information in error messages. Developers should adhere to best practices for safeguarding servers and application frameworks, which include routinely updating software, turning down unused services, and concealing thorough error messages in order to reduce the possibility of security misconfigurations.

Another crucial component of web security is session management. Sessions are used by web applications to keep track of user interactions and save state between requests. Session hijacking and fixation attacks, in which attackers steal or alter session IDs to pose as users, can result from improperly managed sessions. Developers should employ secure session management techniques, such as employing the Secure option to make sure that session cookies are only sent over secure connections, implementing session expiration, and storing session IDs in secure, HTTP-only cookies.

Along with following these best practices, developers also need to keep up with new security risks and keep learning more about secure coding techniques. Penetration testing, frequent code reviews, and automated security technologies that can spot vulnerabilities early in the development process are all necessary for this. Developers may produce web apps that are resistant to assaults and safeguard users' data and privacy by taking a proactive approach to security.

Furthermore, developers must understand the significance of including security early in the development process rather than as an afterthought as the environment of web development and security continues to change. Developers can guarantee that security features are incorporated into each layer of the web application from the beginning by embracing a "security-first" mentality. This method limits the possibility of exploits once the application is online and lessens the possibility of vulnerabilities being added during development.

The increasing complexity of cyberattacks is one of the major issues developers deal with. It is crucial for developers to keep abreast of the most recent developments in cyber dangers as attackers create increasingly sophisticated tactics. To stop known exploits from being employed, security patches and software upgrades must be installed as soon as possible. In order to minimize the attack surface, developers should also follow secure coding standards, which include eliminating hard-coded credentials, restricting rights to only those that are required, and using the principle of least privilege.

Biometric authentication techniques and multi-factor authentication (MFA) are growing in popularity as solutions to the flaws in conventional password-based systems. Passwords are still essential for authentication, but the shift to MFA offers an additional degree of security. With MFA, an attacker would still have to get past extra authentication elements, such as a fingerprint or a mobile device, even if they managed to get a password. This improves the general security of online apps and significantly lowers the possibility of unwanted access.

Furthermore, new security and authentication issues have arisen as a result of the move to cloud-based services and microservices architectures. The complexities of protecting APIs, controlling access across various services, and guaranteeing safe inter-service communication must all be taken into account by full-stack developers. Identity and Access Management (IAM) products are frequently used in these settings to expedite authorization and authentication procedures across several platforms and systems, enabling centralized user management and enhanced security.

Since a large portion of the logic, data processing, and sensitive transactions take place on the backend API, protecting it is one of the most important parts of full-stack web development. Even if the front end is well-protected, it may still be open to assaults if the backend is not secure. A strong API security plan is necessary, which frequently includes the use of data encryption protocols for both sent and stored data, the application of rate-limiting to prevent brute-force attacks, and secure authentication techniques like OAuth 2.0.

Web application firewalls (WAF) are another area of emphasis because they can be very important in defending applications against many kinds of threats. Between the client and the server, WAF filters, monitors, and blocks harmful traffic in HTTP requests. WAFs can be tailored to identify particular attack patterns, like XSS or SQL injection, and can reduce the likelihood of these flaws.

Developers also need to think about protecting third-party services and guaranteeing their dependability as web apps grow more interconnected. New security risk vectors are introduced by integrations with external systems, such as payment gateways, social network logins, and data storage services. Developers must make sure that each third-party service they connect with follows security best practices, which include secure APIs, appropriate authentication procedures, and encryption of sensitive data.

To sum up, security and authentication are essential to the creation of any full-stack web application. While permission controls what users can do within the system, authentication makes sure that only authorized users can access an application. To protect data and guarantee the integrity of the application, security methods like encryption, defense against common vulnerabilities, and secure session management are crucial. Full-stack developers can produce reliable, safe apps that customers can rely on by following security best practices, keeping up with new threats, and implementing security protections at every stage of the development process.

CHAPTER IV
Connecting Front-End & Back-End

RESTful APIs

RESTful APIs have become a cornerstone of modern web development, particularly in full-stack development. They stand for an approach to creating scalable, stateless, and straightforward web services. Representational State Transfer, or REST for short, is an architectural style as opposed to a protocol. RESTful APIs operate on resources, including data, which are usually expressed in formats like JSON or XML using HTTP methods. RESTful APIs are frequently used by full-stack developers to build apps with seamless client-side and server-side communication. As long as both parties follow the same API contracts, this division of responsibilities makes it simpler to design and maintain online applications.

RESTful APIs make it easier to connect the many parts of a web application in full-stack web development. To retrieve user data, for instance, the front-end may send an HTTP request to the back-end. The request is processed by the back-end, which is frequently database-powered. It then retrieves the required data and returns it to the front-end, usually in JSON format. This straightforward cycle of requests and responses serves as the foundation for dynamic, data-driven web applications.

Statelessness, the fundamental tenet of REST, states that every client request sent to an API contains all the data required to complete the request. The server does not have to keep track of session information in between requests, in contrast to conventional server-client interactions. Every exchange is separate and unrelated to earlier requests. Because statelessness eliminates the need for server-side session management, it enhances scalability and streamlines the development process. It also lessens the memory footprint of the server, which enables it to handle a lot more requests at once. Statelessness, however, also implies that developers have to handle any client-side session state that may be required, including user authentication token management.

HTTP methods are used by RESTful APIs to specify what can be done with resources. GET, POST, PUT, DELETE, and PATCH are some of these techniques. Data can be retrieved from the server using GET, new resources can be created using POST, existing resources can be updated using PUT, resources can be deleted using DELETE, and partial updates can be made using PATCH. Every one of these techniques works with a resource, which is usually a URL. For example, a GET request to a URL such as /users/123, which might represent a particular user in a database, would yield details about the user with ID 123.

Standard HTTP status codes are encouraged by the design of RESTful APIs to convey the response to an API call. For instance, depending on the issue, a successful GET request may return a 200 OK status code, whereas a failed POST request may return a 400 Bad Request or 404 Not Found. Clients can swiftly comprehend the outcome of their requests and gently manage issues thanks to these defined status codes.

RESTful APIs are frequently utilized in full-stack web development to supply the back-end functionality for progressive web apps (PWAs) and single-page applications (SPAs). JavaScript frameworks like React, Angular, or Vue.js are commonly used to build the front-end of SPAs, while Node.js, Express, or Django are frequently used to build the back-end. These frameworks enable a rich, interactive user experience by exchanging data and initiating actions using RESTful APIs. While the front-end manages the user interface and user interactions, the back-end manages the database interactions, business logic, and other server-side functions of the application.

Another crucial element of developing mobile apps is RESTful APIs. RESTful APIs are frequently used by contemporary mobile applications to communicate with third-party services or retrieve data from back-end servers. Mobile developers can create apps that are more flexible and easier to maintain by separating them from the back-end through the use of RESTful APIs. A consistent experience across platforms is ensured by mobile apps' ability to use the same APIs as web applications.

Scalability is one of the benefits of RESTful APIs. Because they are stateless, each request may be handled separately, which facilitates application scalability by dividing the workload across several servers. In full-stack development, where applications may need to manage huge concurrent user counts or traffic volumes, this scalability is very crucial. By using strategies like rate limitation, caching, and load balancing, RESTful APIs can be built to withstand heavy loads.

Additionally, integrating RESTful APIs with outside services is simple. The REST architectural style is used by several well-known APIs, including cloud storage companies, social media sites, and payment gateways. These APIs can be incorporated by full-stack developers into their apps to add extra features like letting users store files on Amazon S3, make payments using Stripe, or log in using their Google or Facebook accounts. RESTful APIs are perfect for these kinds of connections because of their ease of use and adaptability.

An essential component of developing RESTful APIs is security. Due to their frequent exposure to the internet, RESTful APIs are susceptible to a number of security risks, including man-in-the-middle attacks, cross-site scripting (XSS), and cross-site request forgery (CSRF). Full-stack developers must utilize security best practices to reduce these threats, like encrypting data in transit over HTTPS, verifying and cleaning user input, and putting authentication mechanisms like OAuth2 or JWT (JSON Web Tokens) in place. These safeguards make sure that only people with permission can access private information and carry out server operations.

Versioning is a crucial factor to take into account while developing RESTful APIs. The API might need to be modified as the application develops in order to support new features or enhance efficiency. Modifications to an API, however, have the potential to disrupt present clients that depend on the current version. Full-stack developers should use API versioning techniques to avoid this. An API can be versioned in a number of methods, such as by including the version number in the URL (for example, /API/v1/users), utilizing custom headers to indicate the version, or implementing a more adaptable versioning scheme based on content negotiation. Backward compatibility is guaranteed via appropriate API versioning, which also enables clients to gradually upgrade to newer versions.

When it comes to documentation, developers must give their RESTful APIs thorough, understandable documentation. The available endpoints, HTTP methods, expected parameters, and response formats should all be included in this description. Developers can share interactive API documentation with team members and outside developers by using tools like Swagger and Postman. Good documentation guarantees that an API can be easily consumed by others and lowers the learning curve for working with it.

Another crucial component of developing RESTful APIs is testing. It is imperative for full-stack developers to guarantee the dependability, efficiency, and security of their APIs. The functionality of the API endpoints can be tested using automated testing tools such as Jest, Mocha, or Postman to make sure they operate as intended in various scenarios. Additionally, performance testing is crucial, particularly for APIs that are supposed to manage heavy traffic. To find possible API bottlenecks and improve performance, tools like Apache JMeter or LoadRunner can mimic high loads.

The ability of RESTful APIs to accommodate a variety of data formats—JSON being the most popular—is another important benefit. JSON is perfect for data transmission between platforms since it is simple to understand and compatible with almost all contemporary computer languages. Though JSON is frequently used, RESTful APIs can also support different forms, such as XML, YAML, or even plain text, based on the application's requirements. The adaptability of RESTful APIs in full-stack development is further enhanced by the freedom to select the best format for various use cases.

RESTful APIs are used for more than only retrieving and manipulating data. Complex workflows involving third-party interfaces, such as payment gateways, authentication services, and cloud storage solutions, are essential to many contemporary apps. For these interactions, RESTful APIs offer a standardized interface that enables developers to easily integrate external services. By removing the complexity of direct interfaces with external systems, RESTful APIs simplify procedures such as integrating with payment providers like Stripe, authenticating users using OAuth2, and storing files in Amazon S3.

As previously stated, security and authentication are key considerations when utilizing RESTful APIs. User authentication and permission are frequently necessary for modern applications, particularly when handling sensitive data or services. To secure endpoints and guarantee that only authorized users or systems may access resources, RESTful APIs can connect with a variety of authentication protocols, including OAuth, JSON Web Tokens (JWT), and API keys. Web development requires secure connections, and data delivered over a network should always be encrypted using HTTPS. This guarantees that an attacker cannot read or alter the data, even if they manage to intercept the conversation.

The idea of idempotency is another crucial component of RESTful APIs. Operations that can be carried out repeatedly without altering the outcome beyond the initial application are known as idempotent operations. Because it doesn't change the state of the resource being obtained, a GET request, for instance, is idempotent. Similar to this, PUT and DELETE requests guarantee that the resource is updated or deleted consistently, independent of the number of times the operation is carried out, making them idempotent; because of this characteristic, RESTful APIs are predictable and dependable, particularly in distributed systems where retries or network failures are possible.

The proliferation of RESTful APIs has also led to the emergence of frameworks and tools that facilitate development and boost efficiency. Strong tools for creating, testing, and documenting APIs are offered by API management platforms like Postman, Swagger, and OpenAPI Specification (OAS). Swagger and OpenAPI Specification offer standardized methods for documenting and describing APIs, which facilitates developers' ability to share and use APIs across various teams and projects. Postman enables developers to directly interact with APIs, test their functionality, and automate testing workflows. These technologies improve the development process and guarantee that APIs are easily testable, well-documented, and long-term maintainable.

RESTful APIs' ability for versioning further contributes to their success in full-stack web development. As previously stated, versioning is required to maintain backward compatibility with current clients because APIs frequently change over time. Versioning can be handled in a variety of ways using RESTful APIs, including content negotiation, special headers, and URL path parameters (e.g., /API/v1/). Because of this, developers can modify the API without affecting clients that depend on earlier versions. Appropriate versioning techniques make it possible for an application's front end and back end to change separately without interfering with the system as a whole.

RESTful APIs are also essential for improving the scalability and performance of applications in the full-stack development space. The necessity for effective data processing increases with the size and complexity of applications. The separation of concerns is made easier by RESTful APIs, which let developers improve certain areas of the application without compromising others. For instance, the front end can be tuned to provide a quicker and more responsive user interface, while the back-end can be scaled separately to manage more API calls. This modular approach to application development, where various components can be adjusted for scalability and performance as needed, is made possible via RESTful APIs.

RESTful APIs have certain drawbacks in spite of their many advantages. For example, they are not the ideal option for every kind of application, especially those that call for more intricate data transactions or real-time communication. Technologies like WebSockets or GraphQL can be more appropriate for applications that need frequent updates, such as chat programs or live dashboards. Full-duplex communication made possible by WebSockets enables the server to instantly send updates to the client. In contrast, GraphQL minimizes the over-fetching and under-fetching of data that can happen with

RESTful APIs by enabling clients to request just the data they require.

Existing strategies, such as RESTful APIs, will be supplemented or even replaced by new tools and paradigms as technology develops. But because of their simplicity, scalability, and user-friendliness, RESTful APIs have endured. Full-stack web developers who want to make cutting-edge, data-driven apps still find them to be a strong and adaptable tool. They are essential to full-stack development because of their capacity to scale effectively, support several data formats, and interface with a wide range of services and technologies.

To sum up, RESTful APIs are essential to full-stack web development because they facilitate smooth front-end and back-end communication. They enable programmers to design applications that are flexible, scalable, and maintainable and that readily interface with external services. Full-stack developers can create dependable and effective APIs that serve as the foundation for contemporary online applications by following the REST principles, utilizing security and versioning best practices, and making sure that testing and documentation are thorough. RESTful APIs are an essential tool for creating dynamic, data-driven websites and apps because of their ease of use, scalability, and flexibility.

Data Handling

Building dynamic and effective web apps requires effective data handling in full-stack web development. It entails gathering, storing, modifying, and presenting data throughout the stack to guarantee smooth communication between the application's front end and back end. The term "data handling" in full-stack development refers to the utilization of databases as well as APIs, data structures, and other technologies that improve data flow across the application lifecycle. Because it guarantees that data can be retrieved and shown effectively while preserving the information's integrity and security, effective data handling is essential to developing scalable, responsive, and user-friendly applications.

Knowing how to effectively store and retrieve data is one of the most important aspects of data handling in full-stack development. Databases, which serve as the back-end repository for storing user data, transactional data, and other pertinent data, are used in the majority of web applications. Relational databases and NoSQL databases are the two primary database types that are frequently utilized in full-stack development. Structured query language (SQL) is used by relational databases, including MySQL, PostgreSQL, and SQLite, to define, manage, and work with data in tabular formats. Applications requiring complicated queries, data integrity, and relationships between various entities are best suited for these databases. A relational database, for instance, might be used by an e-commerce application to hold data on goods, clients, orders, and payments. Foreign keys would be used to connect these entities.

However, unstructured or semi-structured data that does not cleanly fit into tabular representations can be handled by NoSQL databases like MongoDB, CouchDB, and Cassandra. NoSQL databases are better suitable for applications that handle massive amounts of data or demand high levels of scalability since they offer greater flexibility in terms of data modeling. Because user profiles, posts, comments, and interactions can vary greatly and don't necessarily fit into the strict structure of a relational database, a social media platform may store these kinds of data in a NoSQL database. The application's needs, the kind of data being handled, and the system's scalability requirements all influence the decision between relational and NoSQL databases.

Making sure the data can be effectively retrieved and altered is the next stage once it has been entered into a database. This is where the application's back-end is useful. Database queries, user input, and business logic are handled by the back-end, which is usually constructed using server-side languages like Node.js, Python, Ruby, or Java. The back-end and database interact in full-stack development via a variety of methods, including SQL queries, ORM (Object-Relational Mapping) frameworks, and query builders. Developers can use object-oriented programming concepts to connect with relational databases with ORM frameworks like Django ORM (for Python) or Sequelize (for Node.js). These frameworks make it simpler to carry out CRUD (Create, Read, Update, Delete) actions on the database by abstracting away the difficulty of performing raw SQL queries. Query builders, on the other hand, offer a more adaptable and lightweight method that enables developers to create SQL queries dynamically in response to application logic or user input.

Full-stack web applications frequently use APIs in addition to conventional databases to manage data transfer between the front-end and back-end. Application Programming Interfaces, or APIs, facilitate communication between various components of an application or even between apps. APIs are commonly utilized in full-stack web development to allow the client-side front-end to request data from the server-side back-end and vice versa. Modern full-stack apps frequently use RESTful APIs, which communicate with resources using conventional HTTP methods like GET, POST, PUT, and DELETE. These APIs return data in forms like JSON (JavaScript Object Notation), which is easy for the client and server to parse, lightweight, and legible by humans. With the help of RESTful APIs, the front-end can change resources, request particular data, or remove database entries without requiring a page reload. This offers dynamic, real-time data changes, which improves the user experience.

For data processing in full-stack web development, GraphQL has become more and more popular as an alternative to RESTful APIs. GraphQL is a runtime for running queries against data and a query language for APIs. By enabling the client to request only the exact data it needs, GraphQL eliminates the over-fetching and under-fetching problems that are frequently encountered in conventional RESTful APIs, in contrast to REST, which necessitates that developers design several endpoints for various types of data. This allows for more effective data retrieval and reduces needless network calls by giving developers more control over the data they receive. When working with intricate relationships between several entities or in applications where clients need to request big volumes of data, GraphQL is especially helpful. Instead of sending numerous queries to various endpoints, a client may, for instance, use a blogging platform to query for a list of posts and the comments that go with each article.

The front end must present the data in an interactive and user-friendly way after it has been retrieved from the back-end. JavaScript and front-end frameworks like React, Angular, and Vue.js are useful in this situation. The DOM (Document Object Model) is altered by JavaScript and its related libraries and frameworks, which also update the user interface in response to information from the back-end. JavaScript, for instance, can be used in social networking applications to dynamically load new comments or posts without requiring a page reload. Because users may engage with the program in real-time, this results in a more seamless and fluid user experience.

Front-end frameworks like React not only provide dynamic rendering but also effective application state management. The information that dictates an application's behavior at any given moment is referred to as its state. Information regarding the current user, the data being shown, or the outcomes of an API request are examples of states in a full-stack online application. The user interface is constantly in sync with the data thanks to front-end frameworks, which enable developers to store and maintain this state in a predictable fashion. React, for instance, makes the application more responsive and efficient by using a concept known as the virtual DOM to track changes in state and update only the portions of the interface that require re-rendered.

Optimizing the application's performance becomes more crucial as the amount of data increases. If data handling is not effectively handled, it can become a bottleneck in full-stack development, resulting in excessive latency, sluggish page loads, and subpar user experiences. Developers can use a variety of optimization strategies to guarantee effective data handling. Data caching is one such method that employs in-memory caches like Redis or Memcached to store frequently accessed data in a temporary storage layer. By serving data more rapidly, caching can greatly enhance application performance by reducing the need for repetitive database requests.

Security is another crucial factor to take into account while handling data in full-stack development. Implementing appropriate security measures is crucial when working with sensitive data, such as financial information, personal information, or authentication credentials, in order to prevent unauthorized access or alteration. This involves employing secure authentication techniques like OAuth or JWT (JSON Web Tokens), encrypting sensitive data while it's in transit and at rest, and verifying user input to stop SQL injection and other kinds of attacks. To guarantee that the application is safe and user data is safeguarded, security best practices should be adhered to across the board, from the database to the front-end.

Additionally, developers need to think about the scalability of their data-handling systems as online applications get more complicated. The capacity of a program to manage growing volumes of data or user traffic without compromising performance is known as scalability. Adding extra servers to spread the burden of incoming requests is known as horizontal scaling, and it is one method of achieving scalability. A large-scale application, for example, may employ load balancers to split up requests among several back-end servers, each of which is in charge of processing a certain amount of the data. Similar to this, sharding—the process of dividing data among several database instances—allows databases to grow horizontally. This guarantees that the application stays responsive even as it expands and enables the system to manage higher data volumes.

The deployment and monitoring of apps are also crucial aspects of full-stack development. After the program goes live, data handling doesn't stop; developers still need to keep an eye on how well it's doing, particularly as it grows. Monitoring tools can be used to keep tabs on database performance, API response times, and data flows in production settings. This enables developers to spot data handling bottlenecks or problems that might not be noticeable during development or testing. Error tracking and logging are essential parts of this process because they offer important information about how data is being handled and where possible issues could occur. Developers can proactively detect problems before they affect the user experience and guarantee that the application functions properly by putting in place appropriate monitoring and logging mechanisms.

Furthermore, managing massive amounts of data effectively in contemporary full-stack web development necessitates a mix of techniques, including data segmentation, sharding, and horizontal scaling. Scaling up the database by adding extra storage or RAM might not be enough to guarantee optimal performance when working with large volumes of data. In these situations, horizontal scaling—which divides data among several servers—can lessen the strain on any one computer and increase the system's throughput as a whole. A common approach in this situation is sharding, which divides the database into smaller, easier-to-manage sections, or "shards." Data is dispersed according to predetermined parameters, like a user ID or geographic region, and each shard is kept on a separate server. In large-scale applications, this method can greatly increase speed and lower the possibility of server overload.

Lastly, two essential components of data handling in full-stack development are monitoring and debugging. Finding problems with data flow, database queries, or API interactions can get more difficult as systems get more sophisticated. To keep an eye on their apps' performance and spot any possible faults or bottlenecks, developers might employ a variety of tools and methods. For instance, logging enables programmers to record specifics about how the application behaves, such as database queries, API requests, and errors. Troubleshooting problems, speed optimization, and application smoothness can all be achieved using this information.

To sum up, data handling in full-stack web development is a complex process that includes controlling the data flow between an application's front end and back end. Databases, APIs, front-end frameworks, data caching, security, scalability, and monitoring are just a few of the many tools and methods it includes. Efficient data management guarantees that web apps are quick, responsive, and safe, giving users a smooth and joyful experience. Learning data handling techniques will continue to be essential for developers looking to create cutting-edge, dynamic, and scalable web apps as full-stack web development develops.

State Management

State management is a fundamental concept in full-stack web development, particularly when building interactive, dynamic applications. Fundamentally, state management describes how a web application monitors and manages the data that changes over the course of its lifespan. This covers everything, including database changes, server responses, and user input. In addition to enhancing performance and user experience, efficient state management guarantees that data moves consistently between the front-end and back-end of an application.

Client-side and server-side states are the two primary types of states seen in a typical full-stack online application. The browser controls the client-side state, which includes information about user interactions, user interface elements, and the status of different front-end components. The server-side state, on the other hand, is controlled from the back end and comprises data saved in databases, authentication tokens, and the business logic that handles the data. Maintaining synchronization between these two states and making sure that modifications to one state are appropriately reflected in the other are the challenges of state management, particularly in a complex application with numerous users and real-time updates.

Managing the user interface (UI) and making sure it displays the most recent information without requiring a page refresh is one of the most important parts of client-side state management. In contemporary web development, JavaScript frameworks and libraries like React, Angular, and Vue.js are frequently used to accomplish this. Without requiring a page reload, these tools offer ways to monitor UI changes and adjust the view appropriately. This idea is sometimes referred to as "reactivity," in which the user interface reacts automatically to changes in state. For instance, the UI is re-rendered to reflect changes made to the associated state when a user interacts with a component or submits a form. Because users don't have to wait for a page to reload, their actions are reflected instantaneously, making the application feel more responsive and dynamic.

However, client-side state management can get more difficult as applications get more complicated. Since the state of large-scale applications may be dispersed throughout numerous components, a more structured approach is necessary to guarantee that modifications made to one area of the program do not adversely affect other areas. State management libraries are useful in this situation. For instance, developers frequently utilize Redux or Context API in React to better manage application state. These libraries offer a centralized repository for the state of the program, which any component of the application can access and change. This makes it easier to monitor how data moves through the program and gives you more control over state changes.

State management in full-stack web development can be streamlined with the use of a variety of design patterns in addition to state management libraries. The "unidirectional data flow" paradigm is one such pattern that is essential to frameworks such as React. Data in this pattern moves from the top-level component (the "parent") to its child components in a single direction. Although each component has the ability to change its own local state, it is unable to directly alter the states of other components. To enable the child components to render the new information, the parent component must instead transmit the modified data as props. Particularly in larger applications with intricate hierarchies, this distinct division of responsibilities facilitates comprehension and data flow maintenance.

In contrast, server-side state management handles data persistence across requests and sessions. This entails managing database-stored data, including transactional records, product catalogs, and user profiles. The data is processed and stored in the server-side state when a user interacts with an application, making sure that it is accessible for subsequent interactions. In order to guarantee safe access to protected resources, the server must control user sessions and tokens, which is another aspect of server-side state management.

Session cookies and JSON Web Tokens (JWT) are two popular methods for controlling server-side state. Small data files called session cookies are kept in the user's browser and enable the server to identify the user throughout requests. Traditional web apps usually employ these cookies to save user preferences and login settings. Conversely, JWTs are frequently utilized in contemporary online applications, particularly in relation to RESTful APIs and single-page applications (SPAs). Because JWTs enable stateless authentication, which eliminates the requirement for the server to keep session data, they are a more portable and safe option than session cookies. Rather, the server can validate the JWT on each request since it contains all the user's information.

Managing data consistency is also necessary for managing server-side state, particularly in microservice architectures or distributed systems. It can be difficult to guarantee that every component of the system has access to the most recent data when an application is made up of several services or instances. To preserve data integrity across distributed systems, strategies like eventual consistency, event-driven design, and database replication are frequently used. Even when the state is changed across several services, these strategies enable the system to maintain responsiveness and performance.

Another crucial component of state management in full-stack web development is real-time data management. Real-time updates are necessary for many contemporary web applications, including social media feeds, live chat programs, and teamwork tools. The program must continuously update the client-side state in these situations to take into account modifications made by other users or external systems. Real-time data streaming from the server to the client is made possible by technologies like WebSockets, Server-Sent Events (SSE), and GraphQL subscriptions. This enables the application to maintain synchronization without the user having to actively refresh the page.

Memorization, the practice of caching the outputs of costly calculations and reusing them when the inputs have not changed, is one of the most widely used techniques for state management performance optimization. This method is frequently used in client-side state management libraries such as React to avoid needless component re-rendering. React can improve efficiency by not re-rendering components that don't need to be updated by memoizing state and properties. In a similar vein, developers might minimize the need to continually query the database for the same information by caching frequently accessed data in memory on the server side. Because database searches can create a bottleneck in applications with huge datasets or significant traffic, this is especially helpful.

Managing asynchronous data and processes is a crucial aspect of state management. To retrieve data, handle transactions, or carry out other functions, a large number of contemporary online apps depend on external APIs or services. In order to prevent problems like race situations, inconsistent data, or user interface freezes, it is necessary to carefully manage the state of asynchronous processes, such as loading data from a server, waiting for an API response, or processing user input. State management techniques like the "Observer Pattern" and "Pub/Sub Pattern," which enable the application to subscribe to updates and react to state changes asynchronously, are frequently used by developers to manage these tasks effectively. This guarantees that the program will continue to function while awaiting the completion of external data or actions.

Moreover, another difficulty that developers have is maintaining global state throughout a sizable, intricate application. As programs expand, various parts frequently require access to the same data, including application settings, user data, or authentication status. Inconsistencies and data duplication may result from this, particularly if every component keeps a copy of the global state. Using a centralized state management system, in which all global state is kept in one location—usually a store or a context—is one way to address this issue. For instance, with React, components may access and update the global state without duplicating or managing it independently thanks to features like Redux or the Context API, which offer a centralized store.

Moreover, resolving errors and failures without degrading the user experience is frequently necessary for state management in full-stack systems. For instance, the application must gracefully handle a failure that arises when retrieving data from an API, giving the user feedback without crashing the entire program. In order to prevent the entire application from failing when an error occurs in a particular section of the state, this is frequently accomplished by introducing error boundaries in the user interface (UI), where components are wrapped in error-catching mechanisms. Furthermore, server-side error handling is essential to guarantee that the program continues to work even in the face of unforeseen problems. Server-side faults are frequently handled via strategies like graceful degradation, failover systems, and retry logic, which guarantee that the application keeps running even when there are brief problems with external services or resources.

State management is essential for enhancing the scalability and maintainability of full-stack web applications in addition to performance optimization and error handling. Managing the state gets more challenging as applications get bigger and more complicated. The application may become challenging to debug, prone to problems, and more difficult to maintain over time if state management is not approached in a clear and organized manner. In large teams with several developers working on the same codebase, this is especially true. These problems can be avoided with a well-defined state management strategy, which offers precise instructions on how the state should be managed, how data should move through the application, and how components should speak to one another.

Modular architecture is one technique to increase state management's scalability. Smaller, self-contained modules that may be independently maintained, tested, and updated make up the state of modular applications. With this method, various application components can change without impacting the system as a whole. To lessen the possibility of one component interfering with another, a full-stack web application with multiple features could, for example, have a state management module for each feature. Tools like Redux, which lets developers design distinct reducers that control particular slices of the state, are frequently used in conjunction with this modular approach.

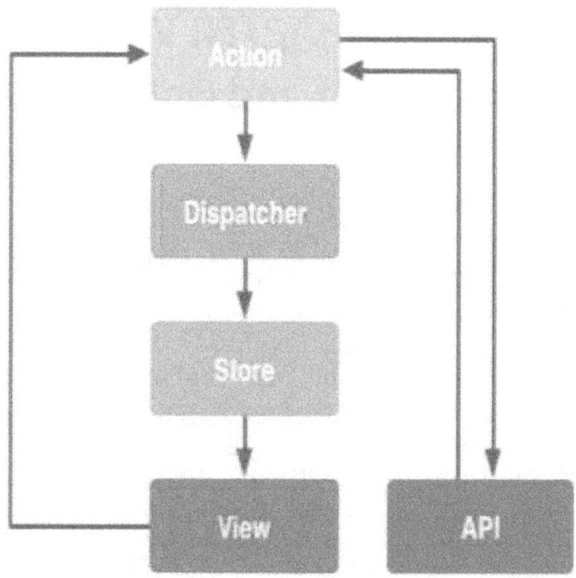

To sum up, state management affects both the front-end and back-end of an application and is a crucial component of full-stack web development. Developers may create scalable, responsive, and maintainable applications that offer a flawless user experience by using effective state management. Building modern online apps requires knowing how to handle states effectively, whether it means handling server-side states with session cookies or JWTs, managing client-side UI states with frameworks like Redux, or guaranteeing data consistency in a distributed system. As web applications get more complex, developers need to stay up to date on the best practices, tools, and design patterns that can help them better manage state and provide users with engaging interactive experiences.

CHAPTER V
Deployment and Optimization

Hosting Platforms

Hosting platforms are integral to the development, deployment, and maintenance of full-stack web applications. Choosing the appropriate hosting platform is essential for full-stack web developers to guarantee that an application functions well, is scalable, and is always available to users. The front-end, back-end, and databases are all saved and made available to end users via the hosting platform. Making educated selections about where to host a web application requires an understanding of the features of the various hosting platform types.

The front-end and the back-end are usually the two primary components of a web application in full-stack web development. While the back-end handles server-side functions, database transactions, and business logic, the front-end comprises the user interface (UI) and client-side components that users directly interact with. The infrastructure and resources needed to run both of these components are provided by hosting platforms. The ability of the program to manage user requests, process data effectively, and scale as the user base increases is guaranteed by a reputable hosting platform.

The kind of application architecture being used is one of the primary factors to be taken into account when selecting a hosting platform. A variety of architectures, such as serverless, microservices, and monolithic, can be used to create full-stack online applications. Different hosting platforms with differing levels of flexibility, scalability, and usability are needed for each architecture.

A conventional web hosting service might be enough for monolithic systems in which the front-end and back-end components are closely connected. However, in order to manage the dispersed nature of the application, more sophisticated hosting solutions are required for serverless or microservices-based architectures.

The technology stack that developers are employing must also be taken into account when choosing a hosting platform. Various front-end frameworks, such as React, Angular, or Vue.js, and back-end technologies, such as Node.js, Ruby on Rails, or Django, can be used to create full-stack web applications. The particular technologies used in the development process must be supported by the hosting platform. A hosting platform that supports Node.js apps and any related services, such as a NoSQL database or a real-time communication service, is necessary, for instance, if a developer is utilizing Node.js for the back-end.

The scalability of the application is also impacted by the hosting platform selection. The ability of a web application to accommodate more users or requests without seeing a decline in performance is known as scalability. Applications can be scaled using a variety of methods provided by hosting platforms, such as horizontal scaling, which divides the load among several servers, and vertical scaling, which increases the resources of a single server. Selecting a hosting platform that facilitates simple scaling is crucial for full-stack web applications that expect tremendous traffic or massive volumes of data. Platforms for cloud hosting, such as Microsoft Azure, Google Cloud Platform (GCP), and Amazon Web Services (AWS), offer flexible scaling options that can automatically modify the resources according to the requirements of the application.

The degree of control and customization that developers require from the hosting platform must be taken into account in addition to scalability. In order to concentrate on developing applications, some developers like fully managed hosting options that take care of the majority of the infrastructure management. Usually, these systems come with integrated capabilities for load balancing, auto-scaling, and monitoring. Heroku, Netlify, and Vercel are a few examples of fully managed hosting platforms that are ideal for small to medium-sized apps and offer simple deployment processes. However, developers who need more control over their infrastructure could choose a dedicated server or a virtual private server (VPS). Although these hosting alternatives offer more customization and flexibility, managing and maintaining the infrastructure takes more work.

The security features that a hosting platform offers should also be taken into account. Web applications are susceptible to a number of security risks, such as unauthorized access, denial-of-service (DoS) attacks, and data leaks. Because they include features like firewalls, secure socket layer (SSL) certificates, encryption, and frequent security upgrades, hosting platforms are essential to the security of web applications. In order to ensure that the application can swiftly recover in the event of a breakdown, many hosting platforms also provide disaster recovery solutions and automated backups. When choosing a hosting platform, security should always come first, particularly when handling private user information or financial transactions.

Because it directly affects the project budget, hosting costs are yet another crucial factor for developers to take into account. Pricing methods vary throughout hosting platforms, ranging from fixed monthly charges to pay-as-you-go alternatives. Developers can pay only for the resources they use with cloud hosting services like AWS and GCP, which usually offer flexible pricing depending on consumption. Applications with varying traffic may find this to be cost-effective. But when the application expands, the cost can mount up quickly, so it's critical to keep an eye on consumption and optimize the infrastructure to prevent wasteful spending. However, while shared hosting services have set prices, they could have speed and scalability issues. Developers should choose a hosting platform that fits their budget and their goals after weighing the long-term expenses.

Support for continuous integration (CI) and continuous delivery (CD) pipelines is a crucial feature of hosting platforms in full-stack web development. A collection of procedures known as CI/CD automates the testing, development, and deployment of web applications. Code changes are automatically tested and deployed to the hosting platform thanks to this procedure, which enables quicker development cycles and more dependable releases. Code updates can be easily deployed straight from a version control system like Git, thanks to integrated CI/CD workflows offered by hosting platforms like Netlify, Vercel, and GitHub Pages. With the help of these platforms, developers may deploy the application to production with little manual involvement, start automated tests, and upload code updates to a repository. For teams working on full-stack apps, CI/CD is especially crucial since it guarantees that the front-end and back-end components are updated concurrently and stay in sync.

Choosing a hosting platform that facilitates smooth integration with many databases and service providers is crucial for developers creating apps that use intricate databases or microservices. Managed database services, such as Amazon RDS, Google Cloud SQL, and Azure SQL Database, are provided by a number of cloud hosting platforms. These services handle database management duties like security, scalability, and backups. As a result, developers may concentrate on creating the application rather than maintaining the database infrastructure. Cloud systems allow NoSQL databases, such as MongoDB,

Redis, and DynamoDB, in addition to conventional relational databases. These databases are frequently used in contemporary online applications to manage substantial volumes of unstructured data.

In the context of contemporary full-stack web development, hosting platforms incorporate a variety of cutting-edge technologies that enable developers to optimize processes, improve performance, and guarantee security in addition to offering the infrastructure for deployment. These platforms are becoming more and more tailored to meet the needs of dynamic online applications that require intricate database, front-end, and back-end interactions. As a result, a hosting platform's functionality goes beyond just storing and retrieving data; it also includes analytics, automation, monitoring, and collaboration capabilities that greatly increase developer productivity.

Furthermore, the development of hosting platforms has been further influenced by the trend toward serverless architectures and microservices. Modern applications that must scale effectively and manage traffic spikes in real time can no longer rely on traditional monolithic hosting solutions. These days, hosting solutions frequently incorporate cloud-native systems like Kubernetes and Docker, which let developers launch apps in isolated containers that are simple to scale, manage, and orchestrate. The deployment process has been completely transformed by these technologies, which offer previously unheard-of levels of efficiency and flexibility.

It is impossible to overestimate the importance of strong logging and monitoring for developers working with complicated systems. Developers may now monitor every facet of the application's performance thanks to hosting platforms' integration of advanced logging tools and performance analytics dashboards. With the help of this data-driven method, performance bottlenecks can be quickly identified and fixed, guaranteeing a flawless user experience even in situations with heavy traffic. Examples of sophisticated monitoring platforms that enable developers to manage resources in real-time and make data-driven decisions to maximize the performance of the application are AWS CloudWatch, Datadog, and New Relic.

The increasing focus on edge computing is another facet of contemporary hosting platforms that merits consideration. Instead of depending entirely on centralized data centers, edge computing processes data closer to the source, such as a local server, an Internet of Things sensor, or a user's device. Real-time applications like gaming, live streaming, and e-commerce benefit greatly from this decentralization of processing since it lowers latency and increases application responsiveness. Because they enable developers to create faster, more effective apps that expand internationally, hosting systems that support edge computing capabilities are becoming more and more popular.

Utilizing a global network of data centers is one of the major benefits of cloud-based hosting solutions. Developers may deploy their apps closer to end users thanks to the data centers located in various parts of the world owned by top cloud providers. By distributing resources geographically, latency is reduced, load times are accelerated, and total application performance is maximized. This is especially useful for apps that cater to a worldwide user base because it guarantees that consumers will always receive comparable performance levels regardless of where they are.

For full-stack developers, continuous deployment and integration procedures depend on the integration of hosting platforms with version control systems like GitHub or GitLab. Because of this synergy, developers can easily push code changes, guaranteeing that updates are deployed automatically and tested instantly. This procedure is further improved by integrating these platforms with automated testing frameworks, which ensure that bug patches or new features are thoroughly tested before deployment. Hosting platforms enable this pipeline of continuous integration (CI) and continuous delivery (CD), which guarantees the development process's dependability and efficiency.

As previously said, security continues to be a top priority for web developers. In a time when cyberattacks and data breaches are becoming more common, hosting platforms have changed to include sophisticated security capabilities. To guarantee data integrity and user privacy, these include multi-factor authentication (MFA), automated SSL certification, and strong encryption techniques. Additionally, a lot of platforms now come with firewalls and DDoS (Distributed Denial of Service) protection built in, which automatically reduces attacks and protects the application and its users.

Modern hosting platforms have responded by providing more flexible and scalable pricing methods, even if cost concerns will always be important when making a decision. Particularly with pay-as-you-go models, developers can scale resources up or down based on the needs of the application, which allows for cost-effectiveness. For full-stack developers working on projects with erratic traffic patterns or seasonal usage swings, this degree of flexibility is crucial. Developers can make sure they are only paying for what they use by optimizing resources based on demand, which lowers hosting costs without sacrificing dependability or speed.

Web hosting solutions need to keep up with the ongoing evolution of web applications. More modular, scalable, and flexible solutions that are suited to the particular requirements of contemporary applications are becoming more prevalent. Knowing these changes and selecting the appropriate hosting platform as a full-stack developer can make the difference between an application that succeeds and one that falls short of user expectations. Developers can choose a platform that not only satisfies the demands of their applications today but also offers the resources and tools required to expand and adapt in a rapidly evolving technological landscape by taking into account aspects like cost, scalability, flexibility, and security. In the end, one of the most important steps in guaranteeing the long-term success of any full-stack web application is choosing the appropriate hosting platform.

In summary, because hosting platforms offer the resources and infrastructure required for web application deployment and maintenance, they are an essential part of full-stack web development. The type of application design, technological stack, scalability needs, degree of control, security features, and cost are some of the variables that influence the choice of hosting platform. While managed platforms like Heroku, Netlify, and Vercel offer simple deployment workflows for developers who would rather not be involved in infrastructure management, cloud hosting platforms like AWS, GCP, and Azure offer adaptable, scalable solutions that are ideal for contemporary full-stack applications. Developers must make sure that the hosting environment satisfies the requirements of the application and offers the tools and resources required for seamless operation and expansion, regardless of the platform selected. Full-stack web apps can manage growing traffic, provide flawless user experiences, and maintain security and dependability over time with the correct hosting platform.

CI/CD Pipelines

The phrase "CI/CD" describes a collection of procedures and resources intended to automate and simplify the

Integration and deployment of code modifications to production settings. By using this technique, developers may update and distribute features more quickly without sacrificing the stability and dependability of their apps. The front-end and back-end of any full-stack program form its foundation, and they must cooperate harmoniously to produce a cohesive and useful outcome. CI/CD pipelines may significantly increase productivity, lower errors, and speed up deployments when incorporated into the full-stack development process.

Continuous Integration, where developers regularly commit code changes into a shared repository, is the first step in CI/CD pipelines. The goal is to prevent problems that could occur when several developers are working on separate aspects of a project by making sure that these modifications blend seamlessly with the codebase. This is particularly crucial in full-stack web development since it guarantees that an application's front-end and back-end components are correctly connected and functioning as a unit. CI enables developers to regularly commit changes to the codebase instead of waiting weeks or months to integrate code. Automatic testing of every commit enables teams to promptly detect and resolve potential problems. To make sure that any new changes don't disrupt the codebase, automated unit tests, integration tests, and code style checks are performed as part of a standard continuous integration (CI) approach.

The pipeline enters the Continuous Delivery phase after the integration step is finished, which focuses on automatically releasing the most recent version of the application to a production-like environment for additional testing and validation. Every code update that passes the automated tests is ready for release into the production environment when Continuous Delivery is used. Continuous Delivery makes sure that changes are prepared for deployment at all times, whereas Continuous Integration concentrates on making sure that changes are properly integrated. Continuous Delivery lowers the possibility of human error during deployment and helps do away with the necessity for drawn-out, error-prone manual deployment procedures. In full-stack web development, this is especially important because both front-end and back-end components must be deployed simultaneously to avoid any possible problems impacting the user experience.

Automation lies at the core of CI/CD workflows. One of the main benefits of CI/CD is that it automates a lot of manual, repetitive operations. Unit testing, linting code, assessing for security flaws, constructing the application, delivering it to staging or production environments, and alerting the development team to any problems are a few examples of these duties. Automation speeds up, improves consistency, and reduces the possibility of human error in the development process. Furthermore, by automating the testing process, developers may detect issues early on instead of waiting for them to become more complex and difficult to resolve. Automation facilitates process optimization and helps avoid deployment problems in full-stack development, which involves intricate interactions between the front-end, back-end, and database.

The version control system, which serves as the basis for the majority of the pipeline's functions, is an important component of CI/CD in full-stack development. Developers may manage many application versions, collaborate on code, and keep track of changes with the help of tools like GitHub and Git. While the CD process makes sure that the right version of the code is sent to the right environment, the CI process automatically retrieves and tests the most recent code from the version control system. The management and deployment of changes become significantly more difficult and prone to errors in the absence of an effective version control system. Version control plays a key role in CI/CD pipelines' ability to monitor changes and oversee updates throughout the stack.

A crucial component of CI/CD workflows is testing. Because full-stack development involves multiple levels of an application, including the database, server-side components, business logic, and user interface, testing can be challenging. Before the application is released, automated testing guarantees that every layer has been carefully examined. To ensure that every component of the front-end or back-end code works as intended, unit testing is usually performed on each individual component. To make sure that the front-end and back-end communicate efficiently, integration testing takes one step further and examines how different components interact with one another. The last stage of testing is end-to-end testing, which simulates how users would interact with the application overall to make sure everything functions as it should. These tests are automated in CI/CD pipelines, which enable ongoing application validation as it develops.

Beyond automation and testing, full-stack web development can benefit from CI/CD implementation. CI/CD pipelines help development teams communicate and work together more effectively. Everyone is using the most recent version of the application since developers are constantly sending their modifications to the common repository when CI/CD is used. This lessens the possibility of integration problems and merge conflicts that occur when developers work alone or just integrate their code at the end of the development cycle. Additionally, the pipeline's automated feedback enables engineers to promptly fix any mistakes or faults before they worsen.

When it comes to deployment, CI/CD pipelines can drastically cut down on the amount of time needed to distribute updates or new features. A CI/CD pipeline can automate the laborious and time-consuming process of getting code ready for production, allowing updates to be released as soon as they are ready. This keeps companies competitive in the market and improves the user experience by enabling them to offer new features and updates more quickly. Additionally, teams are more responsive because of the speed and efficiency of CI/CD pipelines, which enable them to respond to market requests and feedback faster.

CI/CD pipelines give full-stack developers the chance to incorporate more tools and services into their development process. For instance, developers can automatically scan the front-end and back-end code for vulnerabilities by integrating security testing tools. In order to track the application's performance in real-time and make sure that any performance problems are identified early in the development cycle, they can also incorporate performance monitoring tools. Developers can also take advantage of containerization technologies such as Docker, which make it easier to scale and manage programs by enabling them to be packed into portable containers that can be readily deployed across different settings.

A crucial component of CI/CD in full-stack web development is managing deployments across several environments. Applications are usually deployed to various environments, each with a distinct function, such as development, staging, and production. The staging environment is used for pre-production testing to make sure everything functions as it should, whereas the development environment is where developers work on new features and test their code locally. The finished application is deployed and made available to end users in the production environment. By automating the deployment of code to these diverse environments, CI/CD pipelines lower the possibility of errors and guarantee consistency across the development cycle by guaranteeing that the right version of the code is deployed to the right environment.

Managing the CI/CD pipeline itself gets harder as apps get more complicated. The intricacy of full-stack development stems from the requirement to combine back-end and front-end components as well as additional services like databases, third-party APIs, and microservices. Many teams automate the deployment, scaling, and administration of containerized applications across various environments by using container orchestration systems like Kubernetes to handle this complexity. Applications may be readily scaled, managed, and updated as part of the continuous delivery pipeline when Kubernetes and CI/CD tools are used together to expedite the deployment process.

Many CI/CD pipelines integrate with cloud systems, including AWS, Azure, and Google Cloud, in addition to Kubernetes. While the CI/CD pipeline streamlines the cloud deployment process, these platforms offer the infrastructure required to host apps. In order to improve the performance, dependability, and scalability of full-stack web applications, cloud platforms also provide a number of extra services, including load balancing, auto-scaling, and database management, which are simple to integrate into the CI/CD pipeline.

Maintaining and enhancing CI/CD pipelines is becoming more and more of a burden for developers working on full-stack web development. The CI/CD pipeline must adapt to new needs as applications get bigger and more sophisticated, including supporting more than one programming language, framework, or tool. Using modular pipelines, which divide each step of the process into smaller, reusable components, is one method to deal with issues. Teams can add new tools or features to the pipeline using this modular approach without interfering with the current workflow.

In the end, CI/CD pipelines are essential to contemporary full-stack web development. CI/CD pipelines speed up the Delivery of new features and updates, enhance application quality, and free up developers to concentrate on creating new functionality rather than handling tedious manual activities by automating Integration, testing, and deployment. CI/CD pipelines are an essential component of the full-stack development process because of their speed, efficiency, and dependability, which enable developers to produce high-caliber applications at scale and react swiftly to the constantly evolving needs of the web.

Performance Enhancements

Performance enhancements in full-stack web development are crucial to ensuring that web applications are fast, responsive, and scalable. Both front-end and back-end technologies are used in full-stack development, and enhancing the functionality of both components can greatly enhance the user experience. Numerous factors, including network speed, server performance, database queries, code efficiency, and how effectively resources load and display in the browser, can affect a web application's performance. Each of these elements needs to be taken into account by developers in order to produce smooth, effective applications.

Making sure that resources like pictures, scripts, and stylesheets load quickly is the first step in front-end speed optimization. Reducing the number of HTTP requests is one of the first steps in enhancing front-end performance. A browser sends HTTP requests for all the resources it requires, including images, CSS files, and JavaScript files, whenever it loads a webpage. Load times can be considerably shortened by minimizing these requests. This can be accomplished by reducing the amount of requests by consolidating several CSS or JavaScript files into a single file.

Image optimization is another method for improving front-end speed. Since photos sometimes take up the majority of a web page's load time, it's critical to minimize image file sizes without compromising quality. Compressing photos, using contemporary image formats like WebP, and employing responsive images—which dynamically change their size according to the screen resolution of the device—can all help achieve this.

Compressing and minifying HTML, CSS, and JavaScript files is another crucial front-end performance improvement method. By eliminating extraneous whitespace, comments, and other non-essential characters from code, minification helps files become smaller and improves load times. File sizes can be further decreased by compression methods like Gzip or Brotli, which will speed up download times.

Another crucial method for improving front-end performance is to use browser caching. Static assets can be kept locally on the user's device for a predetermined period of time thanks to caching. As a result, returning customers will see speedier load times because they won't have to download the same materials over and over again. To manage how long materials are cached, developers can put up cache expiration headers.

Performance improvements are equally important on the back-end. In online applications, server-side performance is frequently a major barrier. Response times can be greatly increased by enhancing server performance. Database optimization is a popular method for improving back-end performance. Inadequately optimized database queries can lead to sluggish page loads and a bad user experience because web applications frequently rely on databases to store and retrieve data. Developers can solve this by employing effective querying strategies, minimizing pointless joins, and indexing frequently requested columns to improve queries.

Caching is an additional method for enhancing back-end performance. There are several ways to incorporate caching in an application, including server-side caching and in-memory caching. In order to speed up the retrieval of frequently requested data without requiring costly database queries or computations, in-memory caching keeps it in memory. This can speed up the program and drastically lower server demand. In order to speed up the processing of subsequent requests for the same page, server-side caching can save the results of costly server-side operations, like generating a complicated page.

Another useful method for raising back-end speed is asynchronous processing. The server's response time may be slowed down by web applications' frequent need to complete time-consuming operations like processing payments or sending emails. These tasks can be completed in the background without interfering with the main application thread, thanks to asynchronous processing. This guarantees that even while lengthy operations are being finished in the background, the web server will still respond to user requests.

Another crucial factor in back-end performance is scalability. A web application may need to scale to accommodate more users and traffic as it increases. One popular strategy for increasing scalability is horizontal scaling, which involves adding extra servers to spread the load. To prevent any one server from becoming overloaded with requests, load balancers are used to divide incoming traffic evenly across several servers.

Microservices architectures and distributed systems can be utilized to improve scalability and performance for large-scale applications. An application is divided into smaller, autonomous services in a microservices architecture, each of which is in charge of a certain function. More flexibility and better performance are made possible by the independent deployment and scaling of these services.

Network optimization is another crucial component of full-stack web performance. When users and servers are located far apart, network latency can have a big impact on how well an application runs. A common solution to this problem is the deployment of content delivery networks (CDNs). A network of servers spread over various geographical regions is known as a CDN. The CDN reduces latency and speeds up load times by delivering material from the server nearest to the user when they want it.

Web developers can benefit from HTTP/2 or HTTP/3 protocols, which provide better speed than the conventional HTTP/1.1 protocol, in addition to CDNs. Features like multiplexing, which enables several requests to be delivered over a single connection and speeds up page loading, are offered by these more recent protocols. In order to further decrease load times, they also feature server push, which enables the server to transmit resources to the client before the client specifically requests them.

The functionality of third-party services and APIs must also be taken into account by full-stack developers. A lot of contemporary online apps depend on other services, such as social media connectors or payment systems, to offer extra features. However, if these outside services are unreliable or slow, latency may be introduced. Developers need to make sure that these third-party services are performance-optimized and think about employing strategies like request retries or fallbacks to gracefully handle errors.

Performance optimization also heavily relies on security. Data encryption, permission and authentication procedures, and input validation are frequently used to secure web applications. Although these security precautions are necessary, if they are not executed well, they may also result in performance overhead. For instance, developers must balance security with performance because encrypting and decrypting data can be computationally costly. Offloading security-related responsibilities to specialized hardware or services, like hardware security modules (HSMs) or cloud-based security services, is one way to tackle this problem.

Developers can employ a variety of tools and methods to assess and track a web application's performance. WebPageTest, Google Lighthouse, and New Relic are examples of performance monitoring tools that offer information on how an online application functions in various scenarios, such as slow network speeds or high traffic. These resources can assist in locating bottlenecks and offer suggestions for enhancing efficiency. Developers can also evaluate response times, examine database queries, and keep an eye on server performance via profiling tools. Mobile performance is one area that has advanced significantly in recent years. It is now crucial to optimize web apps for mobile devices due to the increase in mobile internet usage. Compared to desktop computers, mobile devices frequently feature slower CPUs, less memory, and less dependable network connections. Therefore, it's imperative to minimize the load on mobile users and optimize front-end code. By using strategies like lazy loading, which loads only the most important resources first, mobile visitors can be guaranteed a responsive and seamless experience without having to wait for the full page to load.

Improving web performance for connections with little bandwidth is also a crucial factor. Even though 4G and broadband networks are widely available, some users—particularly in poor nations—continue to rely on slower connections. In order to guarantee a positive experience for consumers with limited connectivity, developers must foresee these situations and develop performance methods. For instance, they can utilize responsive design and image compression to provide smaller images depending on the device's bandwidth, use service workers to provide offline functionality, and use data prefetching to minimize the number of queries required during sluggish network conditions.

The complexity of online applications increases along with the demand for effective state management. Keeping a consistent and effective state across numerous components and users is one of the difficulties faced by large-scale online applications. On a single page, for instance, a user may engage with several forms, dynamic content sections, and interactive components. The application may experience problems, including poor response times, incorrect data, or redundant re-renders if state management is not done correctly. Developers can manage and preserve the state of the application more effectively and systematically by using front-end state management tools like Redux, Vuex, or MobX.

Microservices and serverless architectures are becoming more and more popular on the server side. Developers can divide big, monolithic programs into smaller, independently deployable services by using microservices. Each of these services can be grown separately to satisfy demand, allowing for more effective resource use. In contrast, serverless computing isolates the underlying infrastructure, freeing developers from the burden of managing servers so they can concentrate on creating code. Both strategies have the potential to perform better, particularly when it comes to resource allocation and scalability. For example, serverless apps are very effective at managing traffic surges and guaranteeing steady performance since they can scale automatically in response to incoming traffic.

Using appropriate database indexing and query optimization is another essential component of performance improvement. Databases may become a bottleneck as applications grow if tables get too big or queries are not streamlined. In order to minimize latency, developers must make sure that databases are appropriately indexed and that queries are written effectively. Furthermore, data can be divided among several servers with the aid of database sharding and partitioning, preventing any one server from becoming overloaded. Effective database connection management, connection pooling, and making sure the database can scale horizontally to handle massive data volumes are all becoming more and more crucial as online applications expand.

Performance improvements extend to testing in addition to code and architecture optimization. To make sure an application runs smoothly under load, performance testing is crucial. Applications can be stress-tested to find possible flaws using tools like Google's Lighthouse, Apache JMeter, and LoadRunner, which can mimic actual traffic situations. Whether it's sluggish database queries, ineffective code, or problems with third-party services, these tests can assist developers in identifying areas that require optimization. A continuous integration pipeline should include regular performance testing to make sure that adding new features doesn't cause performance to deteriorate.

When optimizing for performance, developers must also consider user experience (UX). It's simple to concentrate only on response times and sheer speed, but user satisfaction is also crucial. For instance, even when a page loads rapidly, it's crucial that the user engage with it right away instead of having to wait for all the parts to load. Although the underlying data is still being fetched, techniques such as skeleton panels, which display a placeholder while content loads, might give consumers the impression that the application is responsive.

Lastly, optimizing performance is a continuous activity. Developers must constantly evaluate and enhance their applications' performance as web technology and user expectations change. Maintaining a high-performance online application requires keeping up with the frequent introduction of new tools, frameworks, and methodologies. Furthermore, as new features are added, performance may deteriorate over time; therefore, frequent performance assessments and optimization initiatives are required to guarantee that the program stays quick and effective.

To sum up, full-stack web development performance improvements are essential to producing scalable, responsive, and quick web apps. Developers can decrease server load, speed up load times, and improve user experience by optimizing both front-end and back-end components. Performance improvement requires the use of strategies including resource minification, picture optimization, database query optimization, caching, and asynchronous processing. Moreover, network optimizations, third-party service optimizations, and scaling tactics all help to boost overall speed. Additionally, developers must employ monitoring tools to track and enhance application performance while avoiding performance overhead and concentrating on security. In the end, performance optimization is a continuing process that necessitates constant focus and adjustment to new user requirements and technological advancements.

CHAPTER VI
Building a Full Stack Project

Project Planning

Project planning is a critical phase in full-stack web development that sets the foundation for a successful project. It includes establishing objectives, comprehending user needs, allocating resources, establishing deadlines, and making sure the procedure stays effective and in line with the final objective. Because of their complexity, full-stack web development projects necessitate careful planning and strategic vision. Project planning's primary goal is to outline the entire development process so that all parties involved—developers, designers, and clients—are in agreement from the start.

Determining the project's scope is one of the first stages of project planning. This entails comprehending the client's or end users' needs and converting them into particular features for the web application's front end and back end. The breadth of full-stack development encompasses everything from database administration and server-side functionality to user interface (UI) and user experience (UX) design. A clearly defined project scope helps prevent feature creep, which can throw off schedules and result in cost overruns and guarantees that the development process proceeds in a specified direction.

Selecting the appropriate technology stack is the next crucial step in project planning. The technology stack in full-stack development is the collection of databases, tools, frameworks, libraries, and programming languages used to create an application's front end and back end.

Time restrictions, developer experience, scalability requirements, and project objectives all play a role in choosing the right stack. To choose a stack that fits the project's technical objectives and end users' expectations, a comprehensive grasp of these variables is required.

Making a timeline or schedule for the project is another aspect of planning. Timelines are crucial for maintaining project focus and guaranteeing that all tasks are finished on schedule. There are several steps in the full-stack web development process, and each one calls for close attention to detail. These phases usually include front-end and back-end development, testing, deployment, maintenance, and preliminary planning and design. Different skill sets and resources are needed for each of these stages, and organizing the schedule guarantees that all jobs are finished in a sensible and effective order.

Determining each team member's tasks and responsibilities is also a crucial step in the planning process. Teams working on full-stack development usually include UI/UX designers, front-end and back-end developers, and occasionally DevOps engineers. By clearly outlining each member's position, the team can function as a unit and prevent miscommunications or responsibility overlaps. Overseeing the planning and development procedures, making sure that tasks are assigned correctly, and maintaining team motivation and deadline focus are all critical responsibilities of the project manager.

An additional crucial component of project planning is risk management. Due to their inherent complexity, full-stack web development projects are susceptible to a variety of hazards, including personnel concerns, client requirement changes, and technical difficulties. Early risk identification in the planning phase is part of risk management, as is the development of mitigation techniques to lessen the possibility or impact of such risks. Regular risk assessments should be carried out during the project, and any necessary modifications should be made to keep it on course.

Managing team communication is one of the most difficult aspects of organizing a full-stack development project. Both the front-end and back-end teams, along with designers and other stakeholders, must contribute to and work together on full-stack projects. Early in the development cycle, communication must be open and continuous in order to address any possible problems. Project management software and version control systems like Git are examples of collaborative technologies that can help improve communication and make sure that everyone is informed of the project's status and any modifications.

Another crucial stage in the project planning process is testing. Including testing time in the project schedule is essential. Testing guarantees that there are no significant errors or problems and that every part of the program functions as intended. Comprehensive testing, including functional, performance, security, and user acceptability testing (UAT), is necessary for both the front-end and back-end. Setting up testing settings, selecting suitable testing instruments, and determining success criteria are all part of testing planning. The application's quality might be jeopardized without adequate testing, which could cause problems later.

Another essential element of project planning is budgeting. The cost of full-stack web development projects can vary significantly based on the project's size, the intricacy of the technologies being employed, and the length of time needed to complete the development. To prevent unforeseen costs later on, it is essential to make an accurate cost estimate during the planning stage. Costs such as developer salary, software licenses, hardware, infrastructure, and continuing maintenance following deployment should all be factored into the budget. A well-defined budget guarantees that the project stays within budgetary restrictions and aids in the team's better resource management.

For the application to launch properly, deployment planning is necessary. Transferring the finished application to a production environment so that end users can access it is known as deployment. This necessitates making certain that the databases, server, and hosting environment are all appropriately set up and performance-optimized. Setting up continuous integration and continuous deployment (CI/CD) pipelines, making sure there are no compatibility problems, and organizing post-launch monitoring and maintenance are all part of deployment preparation. When planning for deployment, it's also crucial to take scalability and future upgrades into account because the application might eventually need to manage more traffic or be updated with new features.

The project continues after the application goes live. The goal of post-launch planning is to continuously improve and maintain the web application. To make sure the program runs smoothly and to fix any problems that may come up, this step entails routine monitoring. In order to enhance performance or security, maintenance also entails adding new features, repairing problems, and updating software. Future versions of the application, including the addition of new features or integration with other technologies, should also be considered during the planning phase. To make sure the app is usable and continues to satisfy users' changing demands, clear post-launch objectives should be set.

In full-stack web development, project planning is a continuous process that calls for adaptability, meticulousness, and the capacity to foresee possible obstacles. It establishes the framework for all development efforts and determines the direction the project will take. Proper planning guarantees that the project stays organized, efficient, and in line with the demands of the client and end users, even though it might be time-consuming and involve a significant amount of upfront effort. Although full-stack development projects can be challenging, teams can overcome obstacles and produce high-caliber, useful web applications that either match or surpass expectations if they have a well-executed project plan. In addition to helping a project be completed on schedule and successfully, good project planning also reduces risks, promotes teamwork, and guarantees long-term success.

Monitoring the progress in relation to the predetermined timeframe is a crucial part of the execution phase. To make sure the project stays on course, project managers frequently employ agile approaches, such as frequent sprints and daily stand-up meetings. In a full-stack project, front-end and back-end developers must coordinate with one another while multiple teams work on different components at the same time. Frequent communication ensures that the client side and server side of the program work together as intended and helps avoid delays brought on by team misalignment.

Handling the intricacy of smoothly integrating front-end and back-end components is another significant issue during the execution phase. In full-stack development, where both sides of the program must perform seamlessly for the web application to be functional, this is very important. To ensure that data moves smoothly between the client and server, full-stack engineers are frequently entrusted with bridging the gap between these two realms. To make sure the finished product functions as intended, it is crucial to have a thorough grasp of how these components interact and to follow sound version control procedures.

During the execution stage, testing is just as crucial. Completing the development of individual components is insufficient. Testing guarantees that all project components function as a single, coherent whole. Both manual and automated testing ought to be done at every stage of the development process, not just at the conclusion. To identify problems early, testing should be a continuous process, particularly when integrating intricate systems like databases, APIs, and outside services. Unit tests, integration tests, and end-to-end tests are just a few of the testing tools that full-stack developers need to know how to use to meet front-end and back-end testing requirements.

The culmination of all the hard work is the deployment step. The program is prepared to be deployed to a live environment so that users may start interacting with it following testing and improvement. A seamless transition depends on careful deployment planning. In this stage, the hosting infrastructure is set up, servers, databases, and other resources are configured, and everything is scaled to accommodate the anticipated traffic. Full-stack engineers ought to be conversant with the hosting platform and its setup, comprehending the needs of the application's client and server components.

After the program goes live, the emphasis switches to keeping an eye on and sustaining its functionality. Fixing any bugs, performance problems, or security flaws that may appear after people begin using the application is known as post-launch maintenance. A good support plan should be in place, which should include patching security flaws, updating the system frequently, and adding new features to the application as needed. To guarantee that the user experience stays at its best over time, full-stack development requires constant monitoring and maintenance of the application's front-end and back-end. This entails not just resolving bugs but also consistently enhancing the program to satisfy users' ever-evolving needs and the rapidly changing technological landscape.

Furthermore, scalability is a major issue in the post-launch stage. The program may need to manage more users and data as its popularity increases. Scalability should be considered from the beginning by full-stack developers to make sure the infrastructure can accommodate future expansion. To handle more traffic, this can entail enhancing the server architecture, optimizing databases, or adding more resources. It might be difficult to scale an application after launch, so preparing for this possibility in advance can save a lot of time and work later.

Additionally, security is a crucial consideration at every stage of development and does not alter once deployment is complete. Even once a full-stack web application is live, its security needs to be regularly maintained. It is important for full-stack developers to keep abreast of the most recent security best practices and implement them in both client-side and server-side code. This entails doing vulnerability assessments, encrypting critical data, employing secure authentication techniques, and patching software on a regular basis. Security is a continual process that calls for constant attention to detail rather than a one-time endeavor.

To sum up, full-stack web development is a thorough and complex process that requires meticulous preparation, execution, and continuous upkeep. Setting the groundwork for a successful web development project requires careful planning, and a well-executed plan can guarantee that the finished result satisfies the needs of the client and end users. Full-stack engineers have to keep an eye on testing, security, and performance throughout the development process, manage complexity, and guarantee smooth front-end and back-end component integration. Developers can create high-quality web applications that satisfy company goals and offer users value by taking these criteria into consideration. Full-stack developers must continue to be adaptable and proactive as technology develops to stay ahead of the curve in web development and guarantee the success of their projects during and after deployment.

Front-End & Back-End Integration

In full-stack web development, integration between the front-end and back-end is a critical aspect of building a cohesive, functional application. It is the responsibility of full-stack developers to make sure that a web application's client-side (front-end) and server-side (back-end) functions harmoniously to give users a seamless, continuous experience. The areas of the application that users directly interact with, like the layout, design, and general user interface (UI), are the focus of front-end development. The server, database, and application logic that handle requests, process and manage data, and interface with external systems are all part of back-end development, on the other hand.

Because it allows data to move between the two sections of the program and guarantees that user activities on the front end initiate the appropriate back-end procedures, front-end and back-end integration is crucial. When a user fills out a form on a webpage, for example, the front-end gathers the information and forwards it to the back-end server, which processes and stores it. The server then sends back a response to the front end, changing the user interface appropriately. These interactions would not work properly without integration, resulting in applications that are defective or dysfunctional.

Knowing how the two sides communicate with one another is the first essential component of front-end and back-end integration. Usually, APIs (Application

Programming Interfaces) facilitate this connection by defining the ways in which the front end can send requests to the back end and receive answers. Two of the most popular techniques for this are GraphQL and RESTful APIs (Representational State Transfer). The request-response approach of RESTful APIs uses HTTP methods like GET, POST, PUT, and DELETE to communicate with server resources. By allowing the front-end to specify precisely what data it requires, GraphQL, on the other hand, enables more flexible data retrieval and can help minimize the amount of superfluous data sent over the network.

The planning stage of a project is when the front-end and back-end integration process starts. To specify how the application will operate and how user activities will cause particular server behaviors, the front-end and back-end teams must collaborate closely. Usually, this cooperation entails specifying the API's endpoints and routes, the data models that are utilized by both parties and the formats in which information will be sent. To make sure that the expectations of the front-end and back-end are in line, it's critical to reach a consensus regarding the data format, the endpoints that are accessible, and the anticipated server answers.

Ensuring the accuracy and consistency of the data transferred between the front-end and back-end is a crucial component of integration. This implies that both teams must be fully conversant with the data structures, including how they are supplied to the front-end and represented in the database. Because it is lightweight, readable, and parsable, JSON (JavaScript Object Notation) is the most widely used format for data transmission between the two parties. Data in JSON format is frequently returned by the back end, allowing the front-end to dynamically change the user interface.

The integration must then be put into practice when the data structures and API endpoints have been established. On the front-end, this usually entails using JavaScript to send asynchronous queries to the back-end, usually via Axios or the Fetch API. These solutions provide a seamless user experience by enabling the front-end to transfer data to the back-end without requiring a page reload. For instance, the front-end sends a POST request with the username and password to the back-end when a user submits a login form. After processing the request and verifying the credentials, the back-end replies with a status indicating if the login was successful. This response is used by the front-end to update the user interface and display the relevant message to the user.

One essential component of JavaScript that makes smooth front-end and back-end communication possible is asynchronous programming. Because asynchronous programming eliminates the need to wait for a response from the server, the front-end can continue to function. This is essential for developing dynamic, responsive web apps. The asynchronous features of JavaScript, such as promises and async/await syntax, allow the front-end to process and deliver many requests without causing the user interface to freeze.

Error handling is another crucial component of front-end and back-end interaction. Errors should be handled gently by both the front-end and back-end, and the user should receive insightful feedback. For instance, the front-end can provide the user with the relevant error message if the back-end is unable to complete a request because of invalid input. Handling network problems, like when the server is inaccessible, or there is a timeout, is crucial on the front end. Ensuring that error messages are unambiguous and instructive guarantees that the user knows what went wrong and can take the necessary action.

Another important factor to take into account when combining the front-end and back-end is security. There may be weaknesses that an attacker could take advantage of because the front-end and back-end are interacting via the internet. Cross-site scripting (XSS), in which malicious scripts are injected into a web page and run on the client side, is one of the most prevalent security threats. Developers must sanitize input and output to avoid this, making sure that no malicious code runs in the user's browser. Furthermore, it is critical to secure the communication between the front-end and back-end. Usually, encryption is used to do this, such as when data is sent over a network and encrypted via HTTPS.

Two essential components of protecting the communication between the front-end and back-end are authentication and authorization. Users' credentials are transmitted from the front-end to the back-end of an application when they log in. The back-end verifies the credentials and provides a token, typically a JSON Web Token (JWT). After that, the token is saved by the front-end (usually in session or local storage) and added to the headers of subsequent user authentication requests. Through this procedure, the back-end is guaranteed to be able to authenticate the user and grant access to particular resources.

Performance optimization must also be carefully considered when integrating front-end and back-end systems. Reducing the quantity of data exchanged between the front-end and back-end is crucial for enhancing performance because they frequently communicate across a network. Techniques like caching, lazy loading, and data pagination can help achieve this. For instance, the back-end can send a subset of the data when showing a list of items, and the front-end can request more data as needed rather than delivering the complete list all at once. This guarantees that the user may begin interacting with the program more quickly and minimizes the quantity of data delivered.

Another crucial method for enhancing front-end and back-end integration performance is caching. The program can speed up response times and lessen server load by caching frequently requested data. Both front-end and back-end implementations of caching are possible. To enable the application to function offline or with sluggish internet connections, developers might utilize service workers on the front-end to cache assets and data. Caching can be used at many levels on the back-end, such as database-level caching or in-memory caching using programs like Redis.

Making sure that front-end and back-end integration functions as intended requires testing. To ensure that the front-end and back-end components are functioning properly, unit tests, integration tests, and end-to-end tests ought to be created. Individual components, such as the logic in the back-end API or the UI elements in the front-end, are the subject of unit tests. End-to-end tests replicate actual user interactions to make sure the entire program runs properly, while integration tests confirm that the front-end and back-end interact as intended. Full-stack applications are often tested using automated testing tools like Cypress, Mocha, and Jest.

The growing popularity of serverless architectures and cloud technologies has also increased the flexibility and scalability of front-end and back-end integration. Cloud services such as AWS, Azure, and Google Cloud give developers the resources and tools they need to quickly deploy an application's front-end and back-end components. Because serverless computing removes the need to maintain infrastructure, developers can concentrate on writing code while the cloud platform extends the application automatically to accommodate demand. The back-end API can be hosted as a collection of functions in a serverless approach, and the front-end communicates with these functions via the network. Because cloud providers manage the underlying infrastructure, this method streamlines the integration process and enhances scalability.

Microservices architecture is increasingly being used for large-scale applications that need high availability or entail intricate data relationships. A program can be divided into smaller, independent services using microservices, which connect to one another using APIs. Better scalability, simpler maintenance, and more effective front-end and back-end component integration are all made possible by this method. Developers can scale or upgrade certain application components without impacting the system as a whole by isolating each service. This enables greater flexibility and quicker release cycles, which is especially helpful for companies that must publish changes frequently.

It's crucial to think about how to scale the application as it expands after the front-end and back-end integration is finished. Full-stack developers must make sure the integration can manage a growing volume of requests and users without sacrificing efficiency. This frequently entails enhancing server speed, optimizing the front-end and back-end code, and putting horizontal or vertical scaling techniques into practice. While vertical scaling entails increasing the hardware of the current server to accommodate greater traffic, horizontal scaling entails installing more servers to manage more load. Developers may guarantee that the program will continue to run smoothly even as the user base grows by projecting future growth.

In summary, a key component of full-stack web development is the integration of the front-end and back-end. It entails making certain that the application's two sides can exchange data, communicate clearly, and offer a seamless user experience. Collaboration between the front-end and back-end teams, meticulous planning, the use of suitable technologies and frameworks, and consideration of scalability, security, and performance are all necessary for a successful integration. Full-stack developers may produce strong, dynamic web apps that satisfy business objectives and provide value to customers by becoming proficient in the integration process.

Deploying the App

In full-stack web development, deployment is putting all your created components—from the front to the back end—live on a server that people can access. The procedure can be complex and includes multiple crucial processes to guarantee that the program runs as efficiently as possible in a production setting. You must first design your application, test it carefully, and set up the required infrastructure so the work starts long before the deployment phase. Selecting the right environment, setting up servers, integrating databases, and ensuring security and performance requirements are all part of the deployment process.

Establishing a stable and dependable development environment is the first step toward a successful deployment. To replicate a production environment, a developer usually begins with a local development environment and uses tools like Docker, Vagrant, or virtual machines. The application's front-end, back-end, and database layers can be built in local contexts without interfering with the real production environment. By employing these technologies, developers may ensure that the application operates consistently in various settings, improving the effectiveness of testing and debugging.

The next stage is deciding where to host the application when it has been developed and tested locally. The hosting environment significantly impacts the program's behavior and functionality after it is deployed. Numerous hosting choices are available, each with unique benefits and drawbacks. Scalable and affordable online application hosting options are provided by cloud platforms like Google Cloud, Microsoft Azure, and Amazon Online Services (AWS). These platforms make deployment easier by offering Platform as a Service (PaaS) or Infrastructure as a Service (IaaS). Without having to worry about low-level infrastructure specifics or managing hardware, developers can easily set up virtual servers, databases, and networking setups with these platforms.

Furthermore, full-stack application deployment has become more common in recent years thanks to containerization systems like Docker. With Docker, developers can package their apps into containers that contain all the necessary components for the application to function, such as the code, runtime environment, libraries, and dependencies. This eliminates the need to worry about compatibility problems while deploying the application on various servers or settings. Kubernetes, a robust platform for automating the deployment, scaling, and management of containerized applications, can be used to orchestrate and manage containers.

The next big step after setting up the hosting environment is getting the front-end and back-end of the application ready for deployment. This could entail integrating the application with a database, establishing API endpoints, and deploying server-side code to a server for the back-end. You must make sure that the server can grow to accommodate demand and that the back end is geared to manage production-level traffic. To guarantee quicker load speeds, developers usually bundle and minify JavaScript, CSS, and image files for the front end. The front-end code can be made production-ready by eliminating extraneous comments, whitespace, and redundant files using build tools like Webpack or Gulp.

Database administration is one of the most important factors to take into account while implementing a full-stack web application. Databases are frequently used by the back-end to store, retrieve, and manage data in order for it to operate efficiently. Depending on the requirements of your application, you can select from a variety of database types, including SQL (e.g., MySQL, PostgreSQL) and NoSQL (e.g., MongoDB, Firebase). To guarantee that data is constantly accessible and shielded from unwanted access, the database needs to be appropriately set up, performance-optimized, and secured. To guarantee dependable and effective communication between these elements, developers must also establish the proper database connections between the database and the back-end application.

Setting up multiple servers to manage various stack components may be necessary for the deployment of some apps. One server may be used for the database, another for the application back-end, and a third for serving static assets, such as CSS files, photos, and videos. Known as a multi-tiered architecture, this type of design makes sure that every component of the system may be grown separately in response to traffic demands. To increase performance and dependability, load balancing can be utilized to divide incoming requests equally among several servers.

Ensuring the security of the application and the data it manages is another crucial component of application deployment. Every step of deployment should prioritize security since flaws in your program could provide bad actors access to users' private information. To do this, data sent between the client and the server must be encrypted using secure communication protocols like HTTPS. To safeguard the program against online attacks, developers also need to set up firewalls, intrusion detection systems, and other security measures. Using technologies like JWT (JSON Web Tokens), OAuth, or other token-based authentication methods can help safeguard access to critical areas of the application for users. Another crucial component of keeping a safe deployment is routinely upgrading software libraries and dependencies since out-of-date code can expose your application to known vulnerabilities.

Managing version control and continuous integration/continuous deployment (CI/CD) is another important component of app deployment. You can manage changes to your codebase and make sure that alterations can be tracked and undone if needed with version control systems like Git. Platforms like GitHub and GitLab, where your work may be stored and developed collaboratively by a team, are often integrated with Git. By automating the testing, development, and deployment of your application, CI/CD pipelines make sure that problem fixes and new features are seamlessly incorporated without interfering with the live environment. Additionally, these pipelines enable testing in real-world settings prior to deployment, which lowers the possibility of mistakes when the app goes live. Continuous deployment makes it possible to offer new features and updates quickly, while automated testing guarantees that the program works as intended.

Setting up logging and monitoring systems is another crucial component of deployment that guarantees the application's continued functionality and health. App performance metrics, including load times, error rates, and server CPU consumption, are tracked by monitoring tools like New Relic, Datadog, and Prometheus. Developers can react swiftly to problems impacting the user experience or performance deterioration by configuring notifications. Developers can obtain application and infrastructure logs by using logging tools like Loggly or the ELK stack (Elasticsearch, Logstash, and Kibana). Critical information about problems, crashes, or other unexpected behaviors that happen in production can be found in logs. Rapid troubleshooting and debugging are made possible by this monitoring and logging system, which also helps guarantee that the app functions properly after deployment.

Managing the environment variables and secrets of web apps is another difficulty. Third-party service tokens, database credentials, and API keys are examples of sensitive data that must be protected and not hardcoded into the application's source code. Developers can safely store and manage these secrets by using environment variable management tools like dotenv or AWS Secrets Manager. By protecting this data, you can prevent unwanted access to the third-party service integrations in your app.

Developers should continue to carry out routine maintenance after everything is set up and the software is released to make sure it stays current and functional. This entails updating the software, resolving issues, enhancing performance, and making sure the application is scalable to handle increasing traffic. After the app becomes life, the deployment process continues; ongoing monitoring, optimization, and iteration are necessary to guarantee long-term success. Keeping up with the most recent deployment techniques and tools is essential to preserving the app's security and functioning as technologies change.

After implementation, security remains a primary concern. Data breaches, distributed denial-of-service (DDoS) attacks, SQL injection, and cross-site scripting (XSS) are just a few of the vulnerabilities that should be guarded against by a properly installed application. Developers should constantly keep an eye out for any security threats and deploy patches or updates as necessary, in addition to using secure coding techniques throughout the development process. Malicious activity can be identified and stopped with the aid of intrusion detection systems (IDS) and web application firewalls (WAF). It's also crucial to keep dependencies current because out-of-date libraries frequently have known security flaws. To safeguard user privacy and stop unwanted access, developers should also make sure that appropriate access control and authentication procedures are in place, including encrypting sensitive data while it's in transit and at rest.

The back-end infrastructure experiences an increase in load as the application grows and manages more traffic. Database optimization is useful in this situation. In order to guarantee that the database can manage heavy traffic loads without creating a bottleneck, developers must optimize queries, indexes, and database connections. Performance can be increased and the database workload distributed by utilizing strategies like load balancing, replication, and database sharding. To lessen database demand for frequently requested data, data caching techniques are also essential. Redis and Memcached are two examples of caching layers that can assist in guaranteeing that an application stays responsive even when it is heavily loaded.

After the application is deployed, testing continues. Continuous testing, including load, security, and performance testing, aids in locating possible system flaws. After every deployment, automated testing frameworks can be used to verify that important functionalities continue to function as intended. This guarantees that no new defects or regressions will be introduced by any modifications made to the application. Pipelines for continuous deployment (CD) and continuous integration (CI) are essential for automating testing and deployment procedures, guaranteeing that the application is constantly deployable and that problems are found early.

After deployment, user feedback is just as important as automated testing. Users frequently run into problems that developers would not have anticipated, such as bugs that only show up in particular contexts or usability flaws. Developers can identify errors, keep an eye on user activity, and gather feedback that can inform future changes by integrating technologies like Sentry, Hotjar, or Google Analytics. By continuously adapting to user needs, a feedback loop makes sure that the program keeps getting better over time. Having a bug-tracking system in place is also crucial so that developers can promptly fix problems as they appear.

Another crucial component of maintaining the app's functionality is post-deployment monitoring. Real-time information about the application's health can be obtained by monitoring technologies like Prometheus, Datadog, or New Relic. Numerous performance indicators, including error rates, server health. Real-time server and application log monitoring enables developers to spot issues before they affect consumers. Additionally, by configuring alerts for particular performance or error thresholds, the development team can be informed right away in the event of a problem, facilitating a prompt resolution.

After deployment, managing app updates is another crucial factor to take into account. Over time, both the front-end and back-end of a full-stack web application could need to be updated to add new functionality, correct errors, or repair security flaws. Because developers must make sure the update doesn't interfere with the user experience, updating a live application can be difficult. By using techniques like rolling updates, blue-green deployments, and canary releases, developers can implement changes gradually, lowering the chance of failure and downtime. Before releasing the update to the public, engineers can make sure it functions as intended by testing it on a small sample of users.

To sum up, implementing a full-stack web application is a challenging yet crucial step in the web development process. It entails a number of interconnected tasks, including database configuration, infrastructure setup, security assurance, performance optimization, and post- deployment app monitoring. A successful deployment guarantees that the program will satisfy user expectations, run well in production, and grow with the company. Developers may implement web applications that offer a smooth user experience, are safe, and function effectively under load with the correct tools, best practices, and ongoing maintenance. Deployment is ultimately not the end of the development process; rather, it marks the start of an ongoing cycle of enhancements, user input, and updates that guarantee the program will continue to be useful and relevant over time.

CONCLUSION

The book "Full Stack Web Development: Build Seamless User Experiences: Master Front-End and Back-End Development Techniques" has guided you through the key resources, methods, and approaches required to become an expert in full-stack web development. From utilizing HTML, CSS, and JavaScript to create visually appealing user interfaces to using Node.js, Express.js, and databases to build strong back-end systems, you have studied the fundamentals of developing scalable, fluid web apps.

You've discovered how crucial it is to connect front-end and back-end technologies in order to provide responsive and seamless user experiences. You can confidently handle complicated web projects with these abilities, whether they include building RESTful APIs, integrating state management tools, or optimizing performance for deployment.

Mastering individual technologies is only one aspect of full-stack development; another is knowing how to integrate them to produce useful solutions. As you proceed on your development path, keep in mind that flexibility, lifelong learning, and a dedication to creating applications that satisfy customers' ever-evolving needs are the keys to success.

You are now prepared to take on real-world problems, realize imaginative ideas, and succeed in the ever-evolving industry of web development, thanks to the information and abilities you have acquired from this book. Start creating, exploring, and influencing the web's future—the possibilities are unlimited.

Thank you for buying and reading/ listening to our book. If you found this book useful/ helpful please take a few minutes and leave a review on the platform where you purchased our book. Your feedback matters greatly to us.

www.ingramcontent.com/pod-product-compliance
Lightning Source LLC
LaVergne TN
LVHW022058200926
848481LV00003B/968
9798349288425